Greening School Grounds

Creating Habitats for Learning

Edited by
Tim Grant and Gail Littlejohn

NEW SOCIETY PUBLISHERS

Education for Planet Earth

Green Teacher

Cataloging in Publication Data:
A catalog record for this publication is available from the National Library of Canada.

Cover design by Diane McIntosh.
Design and production by Green Living Editorial Design Services.

Printed in Canada on acid-free, partially recycled (20 percent post-consumer) paper using soy-based inks by Transcontinental.

Green Teacher acknowledges the support of the Government of Ontario through Ontario 2000 and the Ministry of Citizenship, Culture and Recreation.

New Society Publishers acknowledges the support of the Government of Canada through the Book Publishing Industry Development Program (BPIDP) for our publishing activities, and the assistance of the Province of British Columbia through the British Columbia Arts Council.

BRITISH
COLUMBIA
ARTS COUNCIL
Supported by the Province of British Columbia

Paperback ISBN: 0-86571-436-3

Inquiries regarding requests to reprint all or part of *Greening School Grounds* should be addressed to New Society Publishers at the address below.

To order directly from the publishers, please add $4.00 shipping to the price of the first copy, and $1.00 for each additional copy (plus GST in Canada). Send check or money order to:

Green Teacher
95 Robert Street, Toronto, ON M5S 2K5, Canada
P.O. Box 1431, Lewiston, NY 14092, USA
or
New Society Publishers
P.O. Box 189, Gabriola Island, BC V0R 1X0, Canada

New Society Publishers aims to publish books for fundamental social change through non-violent action. We focus especially on sustainable living, progressive leadership, and educational and parenting resources. Our full list of books can be browsed on the worldwide web at: www.newsociety.com

NEW SOCIETY PUBLISHERS
www.newsociety.com

Table of Contents

Acknowledgements   **v**

Introduction   **vi**

Perspectives   1

Transforming School Grounds *by Ann Coffey*   2

How Schoolyards Influence Behavior *by Edward Cheskey*   5

The Pedagogical Potential of School Grounds *by Anne Bell*   9

Sowing a School Garden: Reaping an Environmental Ethic *by Janet Pivnick*   12

Getting Started   15

Maximizing Participation: Go Team! *by Stephanie Stowell*   16

Funding Schoolyard Projects *by Marilyn C. Wyzga*   19

Ugliest School Yard Contest *by Tim Grant and Gail Littlejohn*   23

A Step-by-step Planning Guide *by Miriam Mutton and Debbie Smith*   25

School Grounds in a Box: Model-making and Design *by Ann Coffey*   29

Greening High Schools: Leaping Subject Barriers *by Barbara Kerby and John Egana*   34

Greening the Grounds   37

A Diverse Dozen: Habitats for Healthy School Grounds *by Paul E. Knoop*   38

Rethinking Tree Planting *by Henry Kock*   40

Natural Wetlands and Retention Ponds *by Jackie Oblak*   43

Bringing Back the Prairie: Ecological Restoration *by Molly Fifield Murray*   46

Desert and Dryland Gardens *by Janet Fox*   51

Creating a Schoolyard Tree Nursery *by Cathy Dueck*   54

Rooftop Gardens *by Monica Kuhn*   57

Attracting Wildlife   61

Whatever Happened to the "Wild" in Kids' Lives? *by Edward Cheskey*   62

The Foundation of Habitat: Native Plants *by David Mizejewski*   64

Amphibian Oasis *by Heather Gosselin and Bob Johnson*   66

Avian Attraction *by Ken Quanz and Edward Cheskey*   71

Projects for the Birds *by Steven Uriarte*   75

Butterfly Gardens *by Kim Denman*   77

Site Enhancements and Safety   81

Benches, Bridges and Other Beautiful Things *by Gary Pennington*   82

Sun Shelters: Respite from the Rays *by Drew Monkman*   86

Schoolyard Ponds: Safety and Liability *by Sharon Gamson Danks*   87

Discouraging Vandalism in Schoolyard Habitats *by Beth Stout*   89

Composting at School *by Rhea Dawn Mahar*   93

Learning in the Outdoor Classroom   99

The Panther Patch: A K-6 Gardening Plan *by Janice Hanscom and Felicia Leipzig*   100

Creating a Field Guide to Your Nature Area *by Bruce R. Dean*   104

Learning Links for Elementary Classes *by Jeff Reading and George Taven*   106

K-12 Activities for the Outdoor Classroom *by Char Bezanson, Craig Johnson,
  Bill Lindquist and Nalani McCutcheon*   110

K-12 Learning in a Schoolyard Prairie *by Robin Greenler*   114

The Abundance of Nature's Imagination *by Karen Krupa*   116

Math in the Schoolyard *by Char Bezanson and Judy Killion*   119

Exploring Food and Culture through Gardening *by Nicole Thibault*   122

Tips and Tricks for Taking Kids Outside *by Nalani McCutcheon and Andrea Swanson*   124

Service Learning: Connecting Classrooms with Communities *by Mary Haque*   127

Project Support and Resources   129
Index   135
Curriculum Index   136

A note about units of measure

Units of measure present an interesting dilemma to the editors of any book intended to be read and used throughout North America. While Americans are accustomed to inches, yards and acres, it is not unusual to find U.S. science curricula following the metric system. And while Canada, and Canadian curricula, are officially metric, many Canadian teachers grew up with the British imperial system in which an inch is a U.S. inch but a quart is a U.S. quart-and-a-quarter. To muddy the matter further, hardly anyone anywhere knows a hectare from a hollyhock. Our solution to this confusion has been to present both metric and U.S. units of measure wherever we thought it would be helpful for readers to have both. The result is often more cumbersome than we would have wished, but more useful, we hope, to the majority.

Acknowledgements

This book is the offspring of the hands and hearts of more than 200 individuals who have volunteered their time and expertise during the past year.

In particular, we thank the dozens of contributing authors who share in these pages their wide-ranging knowledge, their diverse experience, and their passion for the creation of outdoor classrooms and a new model of education.

We also owe an enormous debt to a group of educators who willingly gave their time to critique the proposed contents of the book. Through their detailed and thoughtful comments they showed us where improvements were needed and suggested many topics which were subsequently incorporated to make this a more complete and helpful resource. We thank the following reviewers:

AUSTRALIA: Nel Smit. **BRAZIL**: Michelle Sato. **CANADA**: *Alberta* - Janet Pivnick, Jeff Reading; *British Columbia* - Bet Diening-Weatherston, Vivien Clarke, Linda George, Denise Philippe, Jeff Stone; *Ontario* - Judy Arai, Michelle Barraclough, Anne Bell, Ann Coffey, Cam Collyer, Vince Fiorito, Deanna Fry, Roslyn Harris, Jan Hartgerink, Donna Havinga, Donna Kelso, Kathleen Kelso, Henry Kock, John Eryl Jenkins, Diane Lawrence, Sandra McEwan, Barb McKean, Paul Nichol, Kitty Strite Gatto, John Tersigni, Herman van Barneveld; *Nova Scotia* - Angelica Solena Feigin, Jill Grandy, Betsy Jardine, Rhea Dawn Mahar, Diane MacGregor; *Québec* - Marie Fortier, Loyola Leroux; *Saskatchewan* - Will Oddie, Elaine MacNeil; *Yukon* - Bruce Bennett. **GREAT BRITAIN**: Tony Kendle, Ko Sendo. **UNITED STATES**: *Colorado* - Scott Gillihan; *Connecticut* - Mary Lou Blanchette Smith; *Florida* - Maria Minno; *Indiana* - Sam Carman; *Kentucky* - David Wicks; *Maryland* - Kirk Meyer; *Massachusetts* - Rich Mason, Mary Rivkin; *Minnesota* - Char Bezanson, Dina Bizarro, Jim Gagnon, Nalani McCutcheon, Suzanne Savanick; *New Hampshire* - Marilyn Wyzga; *New Jersey* - Barbara Fiedler; *North Carolina* - Liz Baird, Rosemary Klein; *Ohio* - Stephanie Cluley, Sabiha Daudi, Maureen Heffernan, Mark Hersman; *Pennsylvania* - Tingle Barnes, Catherine Stephenson; *Tennessee* - Dan Edmisten, Maurice Houston Field, Cindi Smith-Walters; *Texas* - Diana Foss, Karyl Watz; *Virginia* - Carol Heiser, Eleanor Hodges, Lesley Mack, Tom Mack, Jean White; *Wisconsin* - Greg Bisbee, Joy Conway, Babette Kis, Stephen Maassen, Dennis Yockers.

Finally, we want to express our heartfelt appreciation of the efforts of many committed individuals who labored behind the scenes to make this book a reality: several dozen Ontario educators whose letters of support helped us to obtain initial funding from a competitive provincial grants program; the creative team of Tracy Kett and Brad Cundiff at Green Living in Toronto who developed the attractive page design and gave us many helpful suggestions; Chris Plant and friends at New Society Publishers on Gabriola Island who guided us in the shaping of this, our first book; our editorial assistant Lisa Newman; and the many others who have assisted in bringing *Greening School Grounds* to fruition.

Tim Grant and Gail Littlejohn
Toronto

Introduction

by Tim Grant and Gail Littlejohn

Pedagogical theories come and go, but everywhere and always it is innovative and energetic teachers who are the real ground breakers in education. Never has this been more literally true than during the past few years as teachers and students across North America have begun to break ground for greener schoolyards. Tilling the soil, planting a seed, creating a nature trail, feeding the birds — it all seems slightly anachronistic at a time when the real, serious purpose of education, we hear, is to prepare young people to compete in a high-tech, global economy. Of course the real purposes of education are both broader and deeper than this, and as many writers in this collection point out, a great many of them can be met in an outdoor classroom.

This book is not a dig-it-and-seed-it planting guide for schoolyard sodbusters, although it does offer much practical how-to advice. Rather, its aim is to guide teachers through all phases of a school grounds project, from developing a rationale that will win the support of principals and administrators, through redesigning the grounds, to tapping the rich potential of the schoolyard as a place for hands-on, multidisciplinary learning. The organization of the book mirrors this process.

The Perspectives section helps readers develop a cogent argument for undertaking a school greening project; it does so, in part, by pointing to research that overwhelmingly supports the view that such projects offer substantial intellectual, emotional and social benefits to children. The Getting Started section gives advice on organizing a project team, developing a collective vision, and getting the support of volunteers and funders. The middle three sections form the heart of planning and implementation, offering design suggestions and how-to advice on a variety of projects from natural wetlands to butterfly gardens to tree nurseries. Finally, the largest section of the book, Learning in the Outdoor Classroom, is devoted to the myriad and multifaceted educational uses of a school nature area.

As a whole, the book reflects the expertise of more than 40 authors and 75 reviewers, many of them North American pioneers in schoolyard greening. As one might expect, their ideas are creative and often ambitious. Yet any project that aims to beautify and diversify a beast as big and bleak as the average schoolyard will take time, energy, enthusiasm, and usually money — in other words, all the personal resources that tend to run dangerously low on Friday afternoons. That is why, again and again throughout the planning of this book, the voices of the experienced have urged and reminded us to "tell teachers to start small." And so we do, hoping that this book will inspire grand plans but at the same time provide the direction and tools to begin the journey in small, manageable steps. No matter how modestly you begin, you will be enriching young people's lives, strengthening your community, and adding your vision and voice to the most vibrant educational movement currently underway on this continent.

Chuck Heath

Perspectives

 Transforming School Grounds by Ann Coffey
 How Schoolyards Influence Behavior by Edward Cheskey
 The Pedagogical Potential of School Grounds by Anne Bell
 Sowing a School Garden: Reaping an Environmental Ethic by Janet Pivnick

Transforming School Grounds

by Ann Coffey

In the mid-1980s, a crusade to improve the quality of school grounds was initiated in Britain under the Learning Through Landscapes program. Word of its remarkable success soon spread across the Channel to Europe, and rapidly fanned out across the world to grow into an international movement. It was one of those old ideas whose time for renewal had come, and perhaps it has come just in time. Many people are now well aware of the need to protect biodiversity and conserve dwindling natural resources. What has been less obvious is how to rescue ourselves in a hurry when the wheels of change turn so slowly. Enter the simple idea of starting with the ground at our children's feet.

During the past decade, thousands of North American schools have begun to take a good, hard look at their grounds and realize the enormous potential for transforming barren expanses of asphalt and frayed grass into exciting natural spaces for learning, playing, and socializing. Bringing back to life the patch of the planet under us is an extremely hopeful act, particularly when it contributes to and strengthens a global regreening movement. The ripple-effect potential of greening up people and communities by greening up school grounds suddenly makes turning things around seem possible. Even probable.

Outdoor classrooms can embrace virtually anything: habitat restoration and naturalization projects; butterfly meadows, ponds, insect gardens, and shrub hedges that provide food and shelter for small mammals and birds; artistic creations such as sculpture gardens, giant chess boards, wall murals, and pavement paintings; nurseries for native plants; and vegetable, berry, perennial flower, herb, and rock gardens. Bats and birds can be attracted by installing roosting boxes, nesting boxes and feeders. In Britain, keeping animals such as sheep, goats, chickens, ducks, and rabbits is gaining in popularity, and some schools even have beekeeping clubs.

Informal spaces for quiet pursuits can be easily and inexpensively created by using a few rocks and logs for seating and trees for shade. High school students can design their own green social spaces. Checkerboard gardens with alternating squares of patio stones and soil can provide a place for kindergarten and primary children to plant their own small plots. Schools that have extensive grounds can transform lawns into nature trails which can be used in winter for snowshoeing or cross-country skiing. Amphitheaters formed of simple naturalized berms can provide outdoor classrooms for music, dance, and theater. The scope of school grounds

Top: Schoolyard pond, England.
Bottom: School orchard and composters, Toronto, Ontario.

Ann Coffey

Ossington Old Orchard School

transformation is limited only by the reach of the imagination. The more diverse the approach, the greater the potential for integrating all areas of the curriculum.

The choices made by each school will be determined largely by site-specific drawbacks and advantages. A suburban or rural school may have many acres of land available for nature gardens, while an inner-city school may be restricted to rooftop vegetable and flower gardening. No matter how limited the space for greening, it is always possible to maximize its potential by, for example, installing container gardens in corners, growing climbing plants along dull stretches of chain-link fencing, and hanging bird feeders from wall brackets.

But what are the benefits? Is this going to mean an additional workload for teachers? What about the cost, and the health and safety factors? Teachers everywhere acknowledge that enriching students' outdoor learning environment reduces anti-social behavior such as violence, bullying, vandalism, and littering. Physical movement in playgrounds is slowed by "obstacles" in the form of trees in planters, paving paintings, movable building objects, and informal seating arrangements. This child-calming effect has reduced the number of "knock and bump" accidents in paved playgrounds by up to 80 percent. Over the years, decreases in juvenile delinquency have been reported during periods of school and community gardening.[1] Similarly, teachers today report that social stresses in the classroom are diminished when young people are engaged in learning through improving their surroundings. In Britain, research shows that both absenteeism and dropout levels decline as school life grows more meaningful for older students; and teachers and students alike are discovering that hands-on activities in outdoor classrooms make learning more interesting.[2] Creating an outdoor classroom may not actually lessen

Teachers everywhere acknowledge that enriching students' outdoor learning environment reduces anti-social behavior such as violence, bullying, vandalism, and littering.

---

150 Years of Schoolyard Greening

SINCE THE 1850s, there have been several campaigns to transform North American school grounds. Some have focused simply on beautification or providing protection from "the fierce heat of summer and the storms of winter," while others have promoted students' health and the "symmetrical education of the individual." Over the years, the school garden became an outdoor classroom providing spaces to teach math, banking, business practices, mechanical drawing, entomology, chemistry, botany, and physical geography. These gardens were believed to cultivate civic virtues: "the private care of public property, economy, honesty, application, concentration, self-discipline, civic pride, justice, the dignity of labor, and the love of nature." In other words, school gardens helped children to become good, responsible citizens who would contribute to society.

Green Team at work in the school garden, Dufferin Elementary, Winnipeg.

By 1915, children's school gardening was recognized by leading educators as a very important factor in the health and whole education of the child and in making cities more beautiful and habitable. During the 1940s, school Victory Gardens enabled young people to make a contribution to the war effort. However, by the end of that decade, school gardening declined and gardens were replaced by formal plantings of grass and trees, perhaps reflecting a desire for peace and an end to strife. Today we have a compelling new goal for an old practice, that of educating about the need to restore the Earth to health, and of reconnecting with, and learning to work in cooperation with, the natural world. — ***Ann Coffey***

Historical references: Department of Public Instruction for Upper Canada, Toronto, 1857; Macdonald Institute, Guelph, Ontario, 1890.

teachers' workloads, but it changes the nature of the work by taking the pain out and putting the joy and excitement of learning back in.

The economic benefits are less immediately obvious but become apparent over time. For example, rather than going to the landfill, organic waste can be composted and used to restore nutrient-depleted soils; learning about natural cycles can persuade students to abandon non-biodegradable packaging in favor of refillable containers, further decreasing waste and tipping fees; low-maintenance gardens and ground cover can replace energy-intensive, high-maintenance lawns that need annual fertilizing, re-seeding, and aerating; and fostering a sense of ownership can reduce damage to school property. As for costs, many materials and in-kind services may be supplied through community donations and participation.

Not to be forgotten either are the less-quantifiable, long-term health benefits associated with physical activity out-of-doors. Planting shade trees reduces children's risk of exposure to harmful ultraviolet radiation, and trees also help to filter dust and pollutants from vehicle exhaust.

School grounds projects designed to bring nature back into our daily lives are crucial for the long-term conservation, protection and restoration of wild places. Most young people never have the opportunity to experience wilderness, and many living in urban settings have few opportunities to explore natural environments. As visits to outdoor education centers become limited by financial constraints, the danger exists that learning about the natural world will increasingly depend upon printed and electronic materials. Teaching in this way is largely an academic abstraction; it cannot foster the kind of lifelong ecological consciousness derived only from learning through the senses in natural settings throughout childhood. Nature, as it has often been repeated, is our best teacher.

The Bee Club of West Malling Primary School in Kent, England.

If your school grounds are nothing but barren rectangles of hard surfaces and pounded grass, perhaps it is time to take a closer look at the options for changing your children's living and learning environments and for de-paving the way to a better and more hopeful future. There can be no better place than our schools for beginning humanity's greatest task — that of reconnecting ourselves to the natural world. ❧

Ann Coffey is the Coordinator of the School Grounds Transformation Programme at the Canadian Biodiversity Institute in Ottawa, Ontario.

Notes

1   Historical references on school gardening provided by Ann Milovsoroff, landscape architect at the Royal Botanical Gardens in Hamilton, Ontario, as a result of her research on school gardening in the Toronto District School Board archives.

2   Emeer Adams, *Learning Through Landscapes Report on the Use, Design, Management and Development of School Grounds* (UK: Learning Through Landscapes Trust, 1990); *Making the Best of Your School Grounds*, video (UK: Learning Through Landscapes Trust, 1990).

How Schoolyards Influence Behavior

What common sense and research tell us

When I think back to my childhood, I realize how fortunate I was to have a tree to climb in my backyard and a nearby creek and woodland to explore. Later, I mourned the loss of the great willow — a threat to our plumbing, I was told — and of the creek — much safer as a fenced, open concrete sewer, we were told. I was ten years old when the tree was chopped down and thirteen when the creek was channelized; yet I clearly recall the joy and comfort of sitting in my tree eating bread and butter after school, and the mystery and excitement that lured me to the creek and its environs. These were familiar places to forage and play. I knew them well. I have little doubt

by Edward Cheskey

that these experiences contributed to my grief when they were destroyed, and to the value I place on nature as an adult.

As North America increasingly becomes a continent of city-dwellers, forays into natural areas are rarities for most children. One piece of land that children do know well, though, is their schoolyard. They are familiar with its physical structure, its rules and its patterns of use. Considering how much time children spend in schoolyards, this is not surprising. Many elementary students spend 15 to 30 minutes in the schoolyard prior to school commencing, 30 minutes during recesses, and 30 to 45 minutes over the lunch period. By my rough calculations, this amounts to about one and a half hours per day, or approximately 20

"The Refuge," Ridgeway Elementary School, North Vancouver.

Chuck Heath

to 25 percent of the total time at school. By the end of sixth grade, students have spent as many as 1,800 hours, or 257 school days, just in their schoolyard!

For most children this is social time taken up by playing and establishing relationships, developing social and physical skills and values. For introverted children, such time can be harrowing. Most schoolyards offer no respite or solace from chaotic throngs of children, schoolyard bullies, and noise. The conventional perspective of school designers and administrators is that the land around the school should be designed and managed for surveillance of students, ease of maintenance, and team sports. Since avoiding litigation is a primary criterion in schoolyard design, the only physical features in many schoolyards are play equipment, or "creatives" as they have come to be known. These horrendously expensive structures can accommodate only perhaps 20 children at one time. The emphasis on surveillance usually means placing them in large open spaces where there is neither shade nor shelter.

Researcher Robin Moore has noted that traditional playgrounds also tend to discriminate along gender lines. Open and expansive sites favor the aggressive behavior of boys, whereas girls prefer games and "being together."[1] During interviews that I conducted for production of a video on school grounds, a grade five girl whose schoolyard is almost entirely covered in asphalt commented: "If only the girls could have a cubbyhole where we could go and talk, without the boys hearing us." Curiously, and perhaps sadly, this girl's lament invariably brings chuckles from a viewing audience.

Educators have long recognized the value of modifying the designs of primary classrooms by replacing rows of desks with activity centers, time-out areas, and other features that address the cognitive, affective, physical, and social needs of the learner.[2] Yet the traditional design of school grounds has rarely been questioned. There is now mounting evidence that the typical schoolyard design, emphasizing surveillance and team sports, exacerbates discipline problems, promotes aggressive behavior, and renders these places, in which children pass a considerable amount of time growing up, miserable and inadequate.

Nutritionists argue the importance of diet to human health, pointing out to us that "You are what you eat." Could it be that the environment we grow up in also influences who we can be? Research by Marian Diamond and colleagues at the University of California demonstrates that for rats, at least, the environment does have a major influence on "who they are." Her studies have shown that when a young rat is placed in an enriched environment with more toys, playmates, and opportunities to make choices, its brain cortex begins to thicken in just a few days, while the cortex of a young rat confined to an impoverished environment diminishes.[3] Even old rats developed larger brains when transferred to enriched environments. The increase in brain size was still greater in rats placed in a "super-enriched" environment consisting of two large cages connected by a bridge. The rats with the largest brains, however, were those raised in a "semi-natural outdoor environment." Not only did these animals develop the largest brains, but their intelligence, measured by their ability to run mazes, also increased. Diamond's study concluded that the main factor driving these physiological changes in the brain was environmental stimulation.[4]

Although caution is needed in comparing humans to other species, such studies do have scientific merit. Evidence from the developing discipline of environmental psychology demonstrates that surroundings affect the mental and physical state of humans, too. Abraham Maslow, celebrated educator, and Norbett L. Mintz conducted one of the earlier experiments on the effects of surroundings on human mental functioning.[5] Volunteers placed in different rooms were shown photographs of people and asked if the faces showed "energy" and "well-being." One room was like a dingy storage closet; the second "average" room resembled a clean and neat office; and the third room was beautiful, with large windows, indirect light, soft armchairs, and wall hangings. People who were interviewed in the beautiful room found energy and well-being in the faces in the photographs, while those in the dingy room saw fatigue and sickness in the same faces. The responses of volunteers in the "average" room closely resembled those of volunteers in the dingy room. The behavior of examiners who were unaware of the project's intent also varied. They rushed through interviews in the dingy room and complained of "monotony, fatigue, headache, sleepiness, discontent, irritability, hostility and avoidance."[6] That physical environment can also have a profound impact on behavior has been further demonstrated by research conducted on children in schoolyards. Increasing vegetation complexity and structural diversity reduces aggression and violence and appears to promote positive human values.[7] After helping to redesign an asphalt "playground" into a diverse setting with swings, structures, sitting areas, a range of vegetation, ponds, and meadows,[8] Moore concluded that the asphalt "generated more conflict and stress... compared to the more diverse setting which... engendered a more harmonious relationship between children of all types."[9]

Natural features such as trees, wildflowers, vegetable gardens, and water appear to have a positive effect on everyone. Exposure to nature has been shown to alleviate stress and promote health.[10] Many experimental studies have demonstrated that humans recover more quickly from certain illnesses, particularly stress-related ill-

... research on people of different cultures, demographics, and gender demonstrated not only a common preference for natural environments, but also that there are patterns in these preferences.... Sweeping vistas, open water, secluded hiding places, mysterious passageways... these are the environmental features that appear to contribute most to our physical and mental well-being.

ness, when they have regular exposure to nature. One school principal reported that a naturalized area that can be viewed from the staff room and used for barbecues and lunch had greatly boosted staff morale. Whatever the cause-and-effect relationships, there are firm grounds for arguing that greener environments are healthier not only for nature, but for humans as well.

In *The Experience of Nature*,[11] Rachael and Stephen Kaplan describe research on people of different cultures, demographics, and gender that demonstrated not only a common preference for natural environments, but also that there are patterns in these preferences. It became clear to them that certain configurations of space, where nature dominates, are favored by most people, and that these prefer-

ences may reflect our ability to perceive aspects in the environment that favor our survival. The Kaplans describe these preferred aspects as mystery, coherence, and legibility. A bend in a trail which you cannot see around, or a passageway that leads to an unknown but unthreatening destination, are examples of mystery in the landscape. Mystery stimulates curiosity, a desire to find out more — a prime motivation in learning and, ironically, one of the concepts that is intentionally stripped out of most schoolyards and public landscapes. Coherence can be explained as a perception that the various parts of the whole picture make sense and seem to fit. Environments that lack coherence include features that appear out of place. Not only are such places usually aesthetically displeasing, but they also generate a sense of uncertainty or unpredictability. Finally, legibility refers to

how easy an environment is to comprehend. Illegible environments breed confusion. An environment that is comprehensible, yet provides us with choices, makes sense in its patterns and features, begs us to explore, and attracts us by its mystery, favors our survival and growth, in contrast to one that is incomprehensible, boring, or dangerous.

Jay Appleton, at the University of Hull in northeastern England, has identified two other human preferences in landscapes, which he refers to as "prospect" and "refuge."[12] Both are aspects of the environment that support human functioning and favor survival. "Prospect" means a long, sweeping vista. "Refuge" refers to a hiding place where, from concealment, one can see without being seen, and gain information without giving away information. This fondness for hiding places has also been documented by environmental psychologist Mary Ann Kirkby who found that most preschool children prefer playing in nest-like refuges whenever such places are available.[13] Another innate preference, as noted by John Falk, is the presence of water. In his research to assess environmental preferences, Falk avoids showing pictures of landscapes with water: "It is so highly preferred that its very presence will raise preference by an order of magnitude."[14]

Sweeping vistas, open water, secluded hiding places, mysterious passageways... these are the environmental features that appear to contribute most to our physical and mental well-being. Designing all of these elements into an environment such as a school ground is challenging, but not impossible. School grounds have the potential to be remarkable resources that not only meet children's developmental needs and promote contact with nature, but satisfy the requirements of school officials as well. Shaw, and Weinstein and Pinciotti recommend that "complexity, variety, opportunities for interaction as well as privacy and retreat" be incorporated into the schoolyard,[15] but this may be achieved in a variety of ways. Children's natural tendency to be attracted to nature seems to peak in the junior years,[16] underlining the importance of natural areas as well as cultivated gardens in elementary school grounds. Secondary school students lean more toward social interaction; at

A diversity of habitats and features helps to meet students' needs for exploration, imaginative play, and quiet reflection.

this stage, opportunities to talk in comfortable outdoor settings with tables, benches, and shade are the imperatives.

Habitats and features in the schoolyard should not only display diversity, but also invite interactive and hands-on exploration. In his doctoral research, Ray Chipeniuk demonstrated that the unstructured time children spend in nature is a key element in developing an environmental ethic and an understanding of ecology as an adult.[17] Children need opportunities for foraging, collecting things and imaginative play. Interviews with children attending schools where naturalized areas have been fenced off indicate that these restricted or "do not pick" habitats are discouraging and promote cynicism, frustration and even anger among children. Naturalist Franklin Burroughs argues that children need places where they can climb on tree limbs and swing on vines without being told that the plants are hands-off: "Better to let kids be a hazard to nature," Burroughs told a gathering of conservationists, "and let nature be a hazard to them."[18]

Somehow I managed to survive my childhood forays to the creek without drowning and the hours spent on the heavy limbs of my willow without breaking any of my own. I guess my parents trusted me. Perhaps to effect the radical changes needed in our schoolyards, we have to place a bit more trust in children. This does not come without risk, but the risk of doing nothing is much greater. ❧

Chuck Heath

Edward Cheskey is a bird conservation planner with the Federation of Ontario Naturalists in Guelph, Ontario.

Notes

1   Stephen Trimble, "A Land of One's Own" in *The Geography of Childhood* (Boston: Beacon Press, 1994), p. 66.

2   C. Weinstein, "The Physical Environment of the School: A Review of Research," *Review of Educational Research* 49 (1979), pp. 577-610.

3   Tony Hiss, *The Experience of Place* (New York: Alfred A. Knopf, Inc., 1992), p. 38.

4   Hiss, p. 38.

5   A.H. Maslow and N.L. Mintz, "Effects of Esthetic Surroundings: Initial short-term effects of three esthetic conditions upon perceiving `energy' and `well-being' in faces," in *People and Buildings*, ed. Robert Gutman (New York: Basic Books, 1972).

6   Hiss, pp. 39-40.

7   For examples, see M. Harvey, "The Relationship between Children's Experiences with Vegetation on School Grounds and their Environmental Attitudes," *Journal of Environmental Education* 21:2 (1990), pp. 9-15; C. Weinstein and P. Pinciotti, "Changing A School Yard: Intentions, Design Decisions, and Behavioural Outcomes," *Environment and Behaviour* 20:3 (1988), pp. 345-371; and Robin Moore, *Childhood's Domain* (London: Croom-Helm, 1986).

8   Trimble, p. 66.

9   Trimble, p. 66

10 T. Hartig, M. Mang and G.W. Evans, "Restorative Effects of Natural Environment Experiences," *Environment and Behaviour* 23:1 (1991), pp. 3-26; R. Kaplan and S. Kaplan, *The Experience of Nature* (Cambridge: Cambridge University Press, 1989); and R.S. Ulrich, R.F. Simons, P. Losito, E. Fiorito, M.A. Miles, and M. Zelon, "Stress Recovery During Exposure to Natural and Urban Environments," *Journal of Environmental Psychology* 11:3 (1991), pp. 211-230.

11 R. Kaplan and S. Kaplan, *The Experience of Nature* (Cambridge: Cambridge University Press, 1989).

12 Hiss, p. 41.

13 Gary Nabhan, "A Child's Sense of Wilderness" in *The Geography of Childhood* (Boston: Beacon Press, 1994), p. 8.

14 Hiss, p. 40.

15 L. Shaw, "Designing Playgrounds for Able and Disabled Children," in *Spaces for Children: The Built Environment and Child Development*, ed. G. Weinstein and T.G. Davids (New York: Plenum, 1987); Weinstein and Pinciotti, pp. 347-348.

16 T. Bunting and L. Cousins, "Environmental Dispositions Among School-Age Children: A Preliminary Investigation," *Environment and Behaviour* 17:6 (1985), pp. 725-768.

17 Raymond C. Chipeniuk, "Naturalness in Landscape: An Inquiry from a Planning Perspective" (PhD dissertation, University of Waterloo, Ontario, 1994).

18 Nabhan, p. 9.

The Pedagogical Potential of School Grounds

Recent research in environmental education and related fields confirms that school ground naturalization projects can benefit children in a variety of ways. Through hands-on involvement in designing, creating, caring for and using school nature areas, children stand to improve their academic performance and to develop the willingness and capacity to work for the good of the human and natural communities of which they are a part.

by Anne Bell

A study of 40 schools in the United States in which the environment is used as an "integrating context for learning" (*Closing the Achievement Gap*, 1998), convincingly demonstrates the pedagogical advantages of this approach.[1] Of the 252 teachers who participated in the study, the majority reported that when the natural environment was the context for hands-on, project-based learning, student performance improved in the following areas: standardized test scores, grade point average, willingness to stay on task, adaptability to various learning styles, and problem-solving.

Native plant garden at Olympic Heights School, Calgary, Alberta.

Jeff Reading

In *Nature Nurtures*, a comprehensive review of current literature on the potential of school grounds, James Raffan puts forward abundant evidence of these and other benefits, outlining the far-reaching advantages of outdoor, experiential, project-based education.[2] Particularly promising, according to Raffan, is that educators are rethinking curriculum — both the formal, subject-bound curriculum and the "hidden curriculum" of surveillance and control that is implicit in traditional schoolyard design. Teachers are gaining a newfound appreciation for the pedagogical potential of school grounds projects that integrate disciplines, have tangible outcomes, and foster ties with the community at large. For students, active participation in such projects gives purpose, meaning and relevance to learning.[3]

Naturalization projects represent a promising means of responding to calls for pedagogical approaches grounded in nature experience, "ordinary lived experience," and "environmental practice."[4] Indeed, a number of environmental researchers and educators emphasize the need for intimacy and interaction with human and natural communities. They hold such lived experience to motivate students and shape their learning in lasting and personally significant ways. Their recommendations complement those of other education theorists who stress the importance generally of personal relationships and local contexts and histories in promoting active and transformative learning.[5]

In her review of contemporary thinking about outdoor play and learning environments, Sharon Stine concludes that children should actively participate in the creation of these places.[6] Certainly schoolyard naturalization offers opportunities to do so, and even to involve children in the full cycle of planning, design, planting, and maintenance. This means, on one hand, inviting them to participate in decision-making, thus shifting control from teachers toward students. On the other, it entails attending to the processes in which students are involved, recognizing that one of the key benefits of schoolyard naturalization is the possibility for sustained engagement with a place and its inhabitants. Such involvement may contribute to children's empowerment as responsible, contributing citizens who better understand political decision-making.[7]

Many participants in school projects link the naturalization process with personal and societal transformation and with the nurturing of environmental values.

The level of students' involvement, as well as the benefits they derive from it, will vary according, in part, to their age. Research indicates that the diversity added to playgrounds through naturalization projects improves the intellectual, moral, and physical development of young children. For children in middle school, educational benefits are linked to establishing ethical principles, getting along with others, understanding delayed gratification, and building the language and social skills to negotiate a place in the world. For children of high school age, outcomes include greater pride and ownership in learning, improved academic performance, and the creation of a lasting sense of place.[8]

Research in the field of ecological restoration offers further insight into the potential benefits of school grounds naturalization. A number of writers stress the importance of the moral and cultural aspects of restoration in "generating healthy relationships between people and the land."[9] They advocate restoration on the grounds, among others, that it challenges the human-nature divide by affirming a place and a role for humans within nature.[10] They point to the healing, redemptive potential of ecological restoration and to the underlying environmental ethic or paradigm that sets it apart from the dominant patterns of modern industrial society.[11] Despite the difference in scale between ecological restoration and schoolyard naturalization, many participants in school projects similarly link the naturalization process with personal and societal transformation and with the nurturing of environmental values.[12]

Such optimism finds support in recent environmental education research on "significant life experiences." Since 1980, several studies have explored the antecedents of environmental awareness, sensitivity, commitment, and activism among adults. All of this research points to the overwhelming significance of outdoor experiences in nature, especially in childhood.[13] In one study conducted in nine countries, childhood experiences in nature proved to be "the most important single factor by far."[14] In addition, many participants in these studies attributed great importance to adult mentors and formal education. At a time when many students have limited opportunities for regular, intimate engagement with the natural world, these findings underline the importance of childhood experiences in nature and the potential benefits of supporting and validating these experiences through schooling. ❧

Anne Bell teaches in the Faculty of Environmental Studies at York University in Toronto, Ontario.

Notes

1 Gerald A. Lieberman and Linda L. Hoody, *Closing the Achievement Gap: Using the Environment as an Integrating Context for Learning* (San Diego, California: State Education and Environment Roundtable, 1998).

2 James Raffan, *Nature Nurtures: Investigating the Potential of School Grounds* (Toronto: Evergreen, 2000).

3 Increased enthusiasm and engagement are among the prime benefits of experiential teaching methods. See Richard Kraft and Jim Kielsmeier, eds., *Experiential Learning in Schools and Higher Education* (Dubuque, Iowa: Kendall/Hunt Publishing Company, 1995).

4 Phillip Payne, "Embodiment and Environmental Education," *Environmental Education Research* 3:2 (1997), pp. 133-153 (1997); Constance L. Russell and Anne C. Bell, "A Politicized Ethic of Care: Environmental Education from an Ecofeminist Perspective," in *Women's Voices in Experiential Education*, ed. K. Warren (Dubuque, Iowa: Kendall/Hunt Publishing Company, 1996); Anthony Weston, "Deschooling Environmental Education," *Canadian Journal of Environmental Education* 1 (1996), pp. 36-46.

5 See Ira Shor, *Empowering Education: Critical Teaching for Social Change* (Chicago, University of Chicago Press, 1992); Catherine E. Walsh, *Pedagogy and the Struggle for Voice* (Toronto: OISE Press, 1991); Kathleen Weiler and Candace Mitchell, eds. *What Schools Can Do: Critical Education and Practice* (Albany: State University of New York Press, 1992); and Henry Giroux, "Border Pedagogy and the Politics of Postmodernism," *Education and Society* 9:1 (1991), p. 24.

6 Sharon Stine, *Landscapes for Learning: Creating Outdoor Environments for Children and Youth* (Toronto: Wiley and Sons, 1997).

7 See Anne C. Bell, "Storied Experiences of School-based Habitat Restoration," PhD dissertation (Toronto: York University, 2000); Franz X. Bogner, "The Influence of Short-term Outdoor Ecology Education on Long-Term Variables of Environmental Perspective," *The Journal of Environmental Education* 29:4 (1998), pp. 17-29; Penin Migdal Glazer and Myron Peretz Glazer, *The Environmental Crusaders: Confronting Disaster and Mobilizing Community* (University Park, Pennsylvania: The Pennsylvania State University Press, 1998); Lieberman and Hoody, 1998.

8 See Raffan.

9 Eric Higgs, "What is Good Ecological Restoration?" *Conservation Biology* 11:2 (1997), pp. 338-348.

10 William R. Jordan III, "Nature and Culture," *Ecological Restoration* 17:4 (1999), pp. 187-188; John Rodman, "Restoring Nature: Natives and Exotics," in *In the Nature of Things*, ed. Jane Bennett and William Chaloupka (Minneapolis: University of Minnesota, 1993), pp. 152-153.

11 Jean-Marc Daigle and Donna Havinga, *Restoring Nature's Place* (Schomberg, Ontario: Ecological Outlook Consulting and Ontario Parks Association, 1996); Stephanie Mills, *In the Service of the Wild* (Boston: Beacon Press, 1995).

12 Steven Aboud and Henry Kock, *A Life Zone Approach to School Yard Naturalization: The Carolinian Life Zone* (Guelph, Ontario: The Arboretum, University of Guelph, 1996); John Bowyer and Sandra McEwan, "Refocusing Education on the Environment," *Interactions: The Ontario Journal of Environmental Education* 8:5 (1996), pp. 9-12; Henry Kortekaas and Sandra McEwan "A Step Back From the Abyss of Environmental Collapse: Or How Does a Society Step Back From Environmental Collapse? One Small Step At A Time," *Interactions: The Ontario Journal of Environmental Education* 9:3 (1997), pp. 9-13; Jeff Reading and George Taven, "Outdoor Classrooms: The Learning Links," *Green Teacher* 47 (1996), pp. 29-31; *Wild School Sites: A Guide to Preparing for Habitat Improvement Projects on School Grounds*, a Project WILD publication, (Bethesda MD: Council for Environmental Education, 1993).

13 Louise Chawla, "Significant Life Experiences Revisited: A Review of Research on Sources of Environmental Sensitivity," *Environmental Education Research* 4:4 (1998), pp. 369-382.

14 Joy A. Palmer, Jennifer Suggate, Barbara Bajd, Paul Hart, Roger K.P. Ho, J.K.W. Ofwono-orecho, Marjorie Peries, Ian Robottom, Elissavet Tsaliki, and Christie Van Staden, "An Overview of Significant Influences and Formative Experiences on the Development of Adults' Environmental Awareness in Nine Countries," *Environmental Education Research* 4:4 (1998), pp. 445-464.

John Egana

Restoration project at Lely High School, Naples, Florida.

Sowing a School Garden: Reaping an Environmental Ethic

by Janet Pivnick

For most of us the environment is what is around us, separate from human activity. Gardening offers the chance to become partners with nature. The reward is not just the salad from the back step, or the gleaming jar of peaches. It is the process of digging in the soil, starting small seeds, watching an apple tree grow. It is an education in observation, in harmony, honesty, and humility — in knowing and understanding our place in the world. — Robin Leler Jeavons

 A garden is an ideal place for environmental education. While digging around in the earth, children learn first-hand how the earthworm enriches the soil and helps their plants to grow, and thus learn a lesson in interdependence. While nurturing their seedlings, they learn about the water cycle and how the sun fuels photosynthesis and, in turn, the entire food web. Back in the classroom, environmental issues take on new relevance as children learn how chemicals used on plants seep into groundwater, affecting aquatic life and downstream water users.

But learning these facts, whether in a garden or in a classroom, does not make children into environmentalists. Environmental problems today do not stem from lack of knowledge. We can teach students how our actions affect natural systems. We can teach them how to have a more environmentally friendly lifestyle. But unless they feel intimately connected to nature, those behaviors will be short-lived and shallow. Their lives will not have a core of environmentalism in which nature factors into everyday decisions.

To create a long-lasting, deeply held environmental ethic, environmental education must address our alienation from the natural world. It must provide opportunities to develop a love for the land and a bond with nature. Perhaps gardening can help us do so.

Gardening is extremely popular in North America. Why, particularly in far northern regions where the growing season can be as short as two months, are so many people enamored with this activity? Certainly, part of it is the knowledge that they can grow healthier, tastier produce than they could get from a grocery store. Part of it is the feeling of pride and accomplishment in seeing the results of their efforts. But part of it is the ethereal feeling that gardening evokes — a feeling of spirit. Speak to an avid gardener and you will hear terms such as healing, meditative, magical, joyful.

This sense of connection with nature is intangible and this makes it difficult to teach. While a garden can provide a place to nurture this bond, it is not the garden

Illustrations: Paul Papin

itself but rather the atmosphere created that is important. The challenge for teachers is to make the garden a place of nurturing, acceptance and exploration — a spiritual place, not simply an outdoor classroom for the mastery of techniques and numbers. For in order for the garden to have the greatest impact as a tool in environmental education it must be a place for reflection, where students can flourish and grow as well.

Gardening helps students to connect with nature in very profound ways. In gardens, nature calls the shots. If there is inappropriate water, sunlight or nutrients, the plants won't grow. In a garden we must live within the limits of nature instead of forcing it to bend to our will. This requires patience, an ability to listen to nature's wisdom, and develops a respect for nature.

A holistic sense is imbued in a garden, a sense that is lacking in most of our activities and that is crucial to a relationship with nature. I remember having this sense of wholeness brought vividly to life in a course in bioregional agriculture. The instructor was explaining that insect pests may be an indication of a mineral deficiency in the plant and, correspondingly, in the soil. Rather than remove the pest, we need to understand why the insect is there and address the root cause of the problem. Certainly, this was a valuable science lesson, both in chemistry and in interdependence. But it was more than that: it was also a lesson that there is an organic wholeness, a truth to all that happens in the garden.

Gardens give us an immediate and direct connection to our food source. When our food is grown in a faraway land, transported long distances, and sold to us wrapped in plastic in a grocery store, eating itself becomes an experience that alienates us from nature. Growing our own food removes these barriers and restores a sense of connectedness to the vital essence of the land, while at the same time helping us to develop a sense of place within our own bioregion.

Gardening gives students a feeling of accomplishment. When they see the first shoots poke through the ground and the first buds appear, and later when they share their harvest with family and friends, they have a feeling of exhilaration and pride. For it is their handiwork, their decisions, their hard work that have helped to create the bounty they are reaping. This tangible outcome contributes to a feeling of self-worth, the value of which cannot be underestimated in developing a concern for others and for nature.

As a school garden project takes seed, a sense of community develops. Students not only share the harvest, but work together to plan and to tend the garden, making decisions on what to grow and managing problems that occur. This practice of sharing and cooperating with each other can spill over into a more harmonious, more empathetic attitude towards the natural environment.

Gardens are certainly not the only way to develop an environmental ethic in children. But they do have a couple of advantages over other outdoor programs. Particularly important, especially in urban communities, is that gardens are accessible. Teachers do not need to transport their classes long distances in order to connect with nature. Instead, the garden is right in the schoolyard or greenhouse. Second, gardening creates an ongoing relationship with nature. Wilderness experiences can be very profound, but in most school systems they last a week, perhaps two. Then students and teachers come back to the classroom and are at a loss for how to maintain their relationship with nature. School gardens make the relation-

Gardening gives students a feeling of accomplishment. When they see the first shoots poke through the ground and the first buds appear, and later when they share their harvest with family and friends, they have a feeling of exhilaration and pride.

ship continuous, allowing children to see the changes that occur in a natural system from day to day and week to week.

In his book *Nature as Teacher and Healer*, James Swan examines what led some of the most prominent environmentalists to the beliefs they hold: "Almost all the most dedicated ecologists can ultimately trace their passion to an almost mystical love for nature that arises from one or both of the following experiences: early positive encounters with nature, usually in the presence of loved adults, and later transcendental moments in natural places that may have had healing value." It seems that gardening can help to create this mystical love. Perhaps through nurturing the land we ultimately nurture ourselves and heal our own wounded spirits. ◈

Janet Pivnick is an environmental educator in Calgary, Alberta.

References

Jeavons, John. *How to Grow More Vegetables Than You Ever Thought Possible on Less Land Than You Can Imagine*. Berkeley, California: Ten Speed Press, 1991.

Swan, James A. *Nature as Teacher and Healer*. New York: Villard Books, 1992.

Ann Coffey

- **Maximizing Participation: Go Team!** by Stephanie Stowell
- **Funding Schoolyard Projects** by Marilyn C. Wyzga
- **Ugliest School Yard Contest** by Tim Grant and Gail Littlejohn
- **A Step-by-step Planning Guide** by Miriam Mutton and Debbie Smith
- **School Grounds in a Box: Model-making and Design** by Ann Coffey
- **Greening High Schools: Leaping Subject Barriers** by Barbara Kerby and John Egana

15

Maximizing Participation: Go Team!

by Stephanie Stowell

Over the past 25 years, thousands of schools across North America have begun to make use of their schoolyards for hands-on, cross-curricular learning. Approaches differ, of course — a school in the arid midwest may create a butterfly garden while a school in the Pacific Northwest recreates a wetland — but all successful outdoor classroom projects have one thing in common: teamwork!

The initial spark that sets an outdoor classroom project in motion may come from one inspired teacher, parent, or community member. However, for the spark to be sustained and the project to succeed, there must be leadership from a wide variety of stakeholders. The project team is the working committee that oversees the development and implementation of an outdoor classroom. Their tasks are to coordinate site planning, fundraising, publicity, building, planting, and maintenance. The diverse skills and support brought by each member of the project team are invaluable in the overall conception, construction and maintenance of a project.

To ensure a solid foundation, a project team should include representatives from several key groups.

Teamwork and student initiative: the foundations of a successful project.

Students

Student leadership and initiative is the driving force behind any successful outdoor classroom project. The components, structure, and goals should be defined by students, and from the very beginning it is their vision for the school grounds that should be cultivated and thought of as the foundation from which the project evolves.

To foster students' involvement, begin by inviting students to develop a vision for the future use and development of their school grounds. How do they currently use the schoolyard? How would they like to use it in the future? What features would they like to have in an outdoor classroom? Creativity should be encouraged and no idea should be discounted. For example, students at a North Carolina elementary school took an inventory of the current uses, natural areas, and signs of wildlife in their schoolyard, and then translated their findings into a vision of their "dream" schoolyard. One student had noticed a depression filled with water at the base of a small hill and suggested turning the area into a water park complete with slides and waterfalls. While unrealistic, it was a creative idea, and students built upon it by working with school district personnel to turn the area into a storm water retention pond.

Students' creativity can also be drawn upon for community outreach. It is hard to say "no" to a child who is passionate about a project, and student-produced informational flyers, posters, and newsletters will be helpful in seeking in-kind donations and volunteer assistance. Additionally, interaction with the larger

16

community is a valuable experience for students and will serve to strengthen their sense of ownership in the project as community involvement grows.

Educators

The creation of an outdoor classroom should involve as many teachers as possible. As is true with students, teachers' sense of ownership in the project derives from their level of involvement; and the more ownership they feel, the more they will use the site as a teaching tool. As the individuals who are most directly involved with students, teachers are an integral part of any successful project team, serving as mentors, resource aids, facilitators, co-workers, and cheerleaders. They must strike the balance between taking the lead to push the project forward and stepping back to allow for student initiative. In essence, the teacher plays the pivotal role of any team, that of coach.

Recruiting for these coaching positions can sometimes be daunting. Teachers may be overwhelmed with curriculum requirements and feel that outdoor learning is an additional burden or "add-on." Or they simply may not feel comfortable taking students outside. To address these concerns, it is necessary to outline how the project, from its design and implementation to its use as an outdoor classroom, will help them meet learning standards and curriculum requirements for all subject areas. What better way to study the life cycles and adaptations of organisms than for students to watch monarch butterflies emerging on milkweed plants that they have planted? What better way to learn measurement than to map the outdoor classroom on the school grounds? What better place for reading and journal writing than a natural area that students have helped to create? Showing reluctant teachers that creating and using an outdoor classroom are unique and effective means of meeting curriculum requirements may be just what it takes to get them to sign up for the project team.

Administration

The support and participation of school officials is crucial, as they can offer insight into budget concerns, future building plans, liability issues, community relations, and funding opportunities. School officials generally react favorably to projects that improve the school's image, offer cost savings, provide cross-curricular teaching opportunities, and foster student leadership. Showing that your project will meet all of these goals is not difficult. Many organizations that offer supporting resources for school grounds projects have available well-researched documentation of the educational benefits for all involved. More importantly, now that thousands of schools across North America have successfully developed outdoor classrooms, you are likely to find teachers, administrators, or even students in your area who are willing to discuss their experiences. These first-hand testimonials are often very powerful in persuading administrators and district personnel of the value of a project.

Maintenance staff

It is essential to include school maintenance staff in all planning meetings from the beginning of the project and to ensure that they have a clear understanding of the purpose and scope of the project. As the people with the most knowledge of the conditions of your site and the equipment available, they can assist in planning and offer valuable advice on locating and using the tools needed for construction and maintenance. They will also play a critical role in ensuring that newly planted trees and shrubs, and areas intended for natural succession, do not fall under the mower.

One often-expressed concern is that an outdoor classroom will increase work for maintenance staff, but in fact the project should reduce the need for grounds

For the spark to be sustained and the project to succeed, there must be leadership from a wide variety of stakeholders.

maintenance. Successful schoolyard projects involve landscaping with native plants, which are perfectly adapted to the rainfall patterns and soil conditions of the region. Over the long term, the planted areas will require less watering than lawns and they will need no fertilizers, which translates into a savings for the school's maintenance budget and reduced risk of environmental damage. Additionally, many outdoor classrooms have a "no mow" area where students study natural plant succession and meadow habitat. Maintenance staff may find that their upkeep responsibilities lessen as there is less turf grass to manage.

Parents

Parents enthusiastically support projects that excite and stimulate their children and many find their own lives enriched by participation in the creation of an outdoor classroom. Their enthusiasm and resources are valuable assets to be drawn upon during the life of the project. Parents often play the important role of fundraisers, working within the community to secure in-kind donations, grants, and other sources of support for a schoolyard project.

Three generations pitch in to help build benches at St. Matthew School in Regina, Saskatchewan.

To reach parents in your school community, get on the agenda of an upcoming meeting of your parent-teacher association. Bring students, teachers and others to speak about their vision for the schoolyard. Send home a student-created flyer or letter in which students outline their plans to transform their schoolyard. Include in the letter a checklist of the volunteer assistance required and a "wish list" of items the project will need. Many parents will not have time to volunteer on a regular basis, but they may have extra shovels and garden tools in the garage.

Reaching the community

It is essential to include members of the wider community as key players on the project team. Natural resource professionals can offer expertise that may be difficult to find elsewhere, and local businesses and civic organizations can offer technical support, in-kind contributions of materials, volunteers, and, perhaps, grants. You may find assistance from a wide variety of sources such as landscape architects ready for a new challenge, local businesses willing to donate plants and other materials, or garden and civic clubs excited to offer their knowledge and hands-on assistance.

Natural resource professionals bring experience valuable to the planning and development of specific components of the project. For instance, a local wildlife biologist can offer advice on creating a wildlife habitat. A native-plant specialist might help you choose plants to attract migratory birds and butterflies. A local horticulturalist can offer expertise in developing vegetable gardens. Additionally, through their direct involvement in the project and interaction with students, these individuals serve as role models and mentors, opening the eyes of students and others in the school community to new career directions.

All outdoor classroom projects begin with a creative spark in the mind of an individual who knows the value of outdoor learning; but no individual should go it alone. Creating an outdoor classroom requires the vision, the dedication, and the hard work of many people, and taking the time to assemble a dedicated project team is the first and most integral step in any successful project. It is time well spent and will result in a project to be enjoyed, used, and "owned" by students, educators and the entire community. ❧

Stephanie Stowell is the manager of the National Wildlife Federation's Schoolyard Habitats Program in Vienna, Virginia (www.nwf.org).

Fundraising for Schoolyard Projects

by Marilyn C. Wyzga

Fundraising is an essential part of most school grounds naturalization projects. After all, materials and labor are needed to implement the great designs we generate. In years of working with schoolyard habitat programs, I've seen a pattern in the approaches taken by schools that have successfully raised funds for these projects. Successful teachers win the support of their school and "shake the money tree"* by having a plan, targeting their efforts, involving the community and thinking creatively.

To illustrate how these common elements of success can help make a schoolyard habitat vision a reality, I'll refer to two schools that have met with success through innovative means. One is Great Brook School in Antrim, New Hampshire, where two fifth grade teachers, Anne Kenney and Barbara Black, have been at the heart of a model, community-based learning project that has transformed their school grounds. The other is Peter Woodbury School, a K-2 school in Bedford, New Hampshire, where a small committee of teachers headed by Leslie Fredette created an outdoor study area around a large butterfly garden and solved a grounds problem at the same time. Their success can be the key to yours.

The project at Harold Martin School in Hopkinton, New Hampshire, was supported by generous community involvement: seniors donated plants; a landscape designer helped design and build a stone pathway; a stonemason created a wall for small animal cover; and a local orchard donated a native apple tree.

Groundwork: Planning precedes planting

When planning a schoolyard habitat project, it is very tempting to leap at any money offer that comes along. But alluring as it may be, resist the temptation to apply for a grant just because one becomes available. Develop your plan first and then look for funding and materials to meet your goals. Otherwise, you run the risk of letting grants dictate what is valuable to you rather than setting the agenda yourself.

To begin, find at least one true partner among your colleagues. Teammates are invaluable. Next, explore your site. Involve your students in this exploration, and invite them to express their impressions of the schoolyard through drawings, words, maps, and photographs. At the same time, have them generate their visions of a transformed schoolyard. Maintain these records through both the planning and implementation stages. They not only provide a history of the project and serve as materials to draw on when preparing to solicit funds, but they also form the basis of your master plan.

Setting roots: Creating a master plan

If your project is to be sustainable and have lasting impact it needs a good foundation, so take the time to build one. Assemble all the players: students, teachers, parents, community members, administrators, board members and maintenance staff. Work together to write the master plan, a tool that will shape the project and be invaluable later in the fundraising process. Outline your goals, build a budget, and develop a long-range plan. When describing your project, touch on broad themes that encompass your larger vision, and tie them into your school curriculum. For example, you might talk about native plant restoration, landscape naturalization, or transmitting ecological knowledge to the younger generation. This shows greater vision than simply stating that "we want to plant some trees."

New ideas will evolve along the way, so leave room in your master plan for growth and change. Think "sustainable" and "long term," and resist the temptation to draw up final plans too soon or you risk robbing the project of its educational value.

Planning does take time, and may seem like a burden, but it will keep the project on track and moving ahead. As Leslie Fredette points out, "If you start worrying and thinking too deeply [about time constraints], you'll think of thousands of negatives, reasons not to do it." Team participation can resolve your concerns about limited time. Students form the heart of the project, and the plan is based on their vision. They can take initiative for researching project ideas or can work in groups to develop portions of the master plan. Consider the possibility of integrating the proposal writing process into your curriculum. Parents are also valuable allies who can often be relied upon to pull together grant proposals, collect maps, and make phone calls.

Marilyn Wyzga

Alluring as it may be, resist the temptation to apply for a grant just because one becomes available. Develop your plan first and then look for funding and materials to meet your goals.

Cultivating the school culture

An essential component of your team is your school administration. You need the support of your principal, parent-teacher association, school board, and superintendent, not to mention, custodian. "Include those key people right from the start — they have wonderful ideas you haven't even thought of," advises Leslie Fredette.

Demonstrate to administrators that you have done your homework and considered all angles of your project and its implications. Be prepared to address concerns about money, time, liability, parent participation, vandalism and student behavior. The administration will be concerned about standards and curriculum frameworks as well. You can address this by structuring curriculum as a core element of your master plan, showing how standards and frameworks will be met through your project. It also helps if your plan includes solving a known schoolyard problem. For example, the garden plan at Peter Woodbury School also addressed a roof drainage and erosion problem. "It's easy to sell something that will have kids as the focal point, beautify the schoolyard, benefit community, and solve problems," says Leslie Fredette. "Then it's good for everybody."

Planting in your zone: Think locally first

Once your vision is developed, your plan is in hand, and your administrators are standing behind you, you need the "stuff" to bring your vision to life. Schoolyard projects are a community effort, so start by looking to local sources of potential support. Service clubs such as Rotary or Lions may make cash or valuable in-kind donations. Environmental groups, scout troops, naturalist societies and garden clubs may have resources and expertise to share. Use the phone book to locate landscapers, construction companies and nurseries, and approach parents who are in these businesses. Make use of your team's creativity and contacts. Parents may have useful contacts with local businesses and organizations, and there is likely someone in your school community who already has fundraising experience and enjoys strategizing.

In approaching potential donors, it helps to ask for specific items. Businesses may be more responsive if you invite them to be partners in your project. They may offer items at a discount, at cost, or with free delivery. Remember, the worst that anyone can say is "no." If this makes you uneasy, and it may, practice. Practice asking for small things first. Role-play with others on your team. Invite someone onto your team who is already experienced in asking for support. Remember, you are not begging! You are inviting funders into a partnership that will enhance the lives of local children and the environment.

Leslie Fredette describes their project as a "community binder" which has brought together parents and local businesses, both large and small. In one instance, they approached a new retail business just as it came into town. "This was such a positive thing," remarks Fredette, "because they were interested in the children, in the people in the community." For sustained funding, Peter Woodbury School hosts family-oriented fundraisers such as annual ice cream socials and sales of tee-shirts, hats and community cookbooks. Parents are involved in all aspects of planning, organizing, and conducting these events. "They want to be involved," says Fredette. "This taps their expertise. The kids come home with such pride, and their parents think this is worth it."

Branching out: Getting the grants

Beyond local support is an enormous arena of potential grantors. If you are going to write grant proposals, begin by identifying potential funders. When you do, you will immediately run into questions of scale. Do you choose national, regional, or local foundations? Many of the heavy hitters — corporate granting programs and large foundations — "require extra big work and need a really different idea to stand out," as Anne Kenney points out. Smaller grant sources, on the other hand, may require regular reports that might not be worth the grant amount. Weigh the investment of your time against the size of the grant.

Rather than sitting down once a year to write one large proposal, be on the lookout at all times for grant titles or descriptions that match any part, large or small, of your project. In this way, you will avoid banking your whole project on one donor and can creatively match specific funders to specific aspects of your plan. Some may give equipment, and some may give money. For example, the first year of Great Brook's project, the State Council on the Arts supported three artist residencies, including a landscape architect who guided the students in designing their wetland boardwalk. Two grants from the New England Reading Association paid for books, historical photos and maps. The Merrimack River Watershed Initiative provided a computer and water testing equipment. The New Hampshire Preservation Alliance funded an historic walking tour of the town. Anne Kenney remarks that in seeking grants, "I'd say we only struck out twice."

Sustained yield: Tips for successful proposals

A well-developed grant proposal can be used again and again. Many excellent publications provide detailed advice for writing successful grant proposals, but here are several key tips:

Call ahead: Every funding organization has specific requirements and deadlines for applications, and most provide application packets. Call ahead to obtain information about their process and ask for a list of the projects they have funded in the past. This gives you an idea of what appeals to them and what approach may be most effective in demonstrating that your project will provide something they value.

Think like a reviewer: Imagine yourself as a grant reviewer mired in stacks of proposals. What would pique your interest? What would make a proposal easier to read? "We receive an over-abundance of schoolyard beautification proposals," says proposal-reviewer Conni White. "If this is your school's focus, and indeed it's a great first step, make it unique." For example, link the project to new curriculum, include a plan for providing wildlife habitat, or emphasize the use of native plants.

Describe all parts of your project: Often funders want to know how you will continue to support the project once their money has been spent. "Don't try for

Planting trees at Francestown School in New Hampshire. The project was paid for by small fundraisers, including a sale of flowers that students had grown in the classroom.

Marilyn Wyzga

the million dollar project right out of the gate," recommends White. "Show a progression of steps so we know you have an investment in the idea." Include a budget that lists in-kind donations of goods and services. This shows you are resourceful and that other people have found the project worthwhile.

Follow the rules: Be brief and to the point and use clear headings to make the proposal easier to read. Include all the information and documentation necessary, but do not include anything that is not asked for. Make sure your copies are clean and legible. Finally, don't wait until the last minute to prepare your proposal; often, your lack of preparation and organization will be obvious.

Follow up: Follow up with funders whether or not your proposal is accepted. They can give you feedback on ways to adjust your proposal to increase your chances of success the next time.

Marilyn Wyzga

Remember, you are not begging! You are inviting funders into a partnership that will enhance the lives of children and the environment.

Reaping the harvest: Success breeds success

When one local company funded Great Brook School, they showed up at the school like Publishers' Clearinghouse, carting a big check — six feet long. The teachers posted it on the bulletin board in the main hallway where it was highly visible, attracting attention and reminding everyone in the school that this was a project worth supporting. Money draws money, and success breeds success. "You can always start small; excitement catches," says Fredette. "Once you've built your reputation and people see how others value your project, they will get involved, too.

In undertaking any schoolyard project, it is important to view fundraising as an essential part of the larger whole. Like planning, researching, planting and building, it is a task in which the entire school community can participate. It is also a potentially rich educational experience that can be incorporated into your curriculum. Fundraising is more than a means to an end. It's a process that parallels your growing project. Be creative, take your time, and give that process room to breathe. Your reward: the results will be richer and your project more sustainable. ❧

Marilyn C. Wyzga is the author of Homes for Wildlife: A Planning Guide for Habitat Enhancement on School Grounds *and the creator and coordinator of Project HOME, sponsored by the New Hampshire Fish and Game Department.*

---

* After the title of Thomas G. Dunn's *How to Shake the Money Tree: Creative Fund-Raising for Today's Nonprofit Organizations* (London: Penguin, 1988, out of print).

References

Lucas, Bill and Anne Mountfield. *A Guide to Fundraising for School Grounds.* UK: Learning Through Landscapes, 1995. Distributed in North America by Green Brick Road, (800) 473-3638, http://gbr.org.

North American Association for Environmental Education and U.S. Environmental Protection Agency Education Division. *Grant Funding for Your Environmental Education Program: Strategies and Options* Washington, DC: NAAEE, 1993. Available from NAAEE Publications, 410 Tarvin Road, Rock Spring, GA 30739, (706) 764-2926, www.naaee.org.

Ugliest School Yard Contest

T he competition was hideous, but in the spring of 1998, St. Anthony School in Ottawa beat out its desolate running mates to claim the dubious distinction of having the ugliest schoolyard in town. As the winner of the first-anywhere Ugliest School Yard Contest, the school was awarded $5,000 to spend on plants and materials for greening the school grounds, and assisted by staff of the Canadian Institute of Biodiversity in planning and implementing the project.

by Tim Grant and Gail Littlejohn

But beyond the obvious benefit to students and staff at St. Anthony School, the Ugliest School Yard Contest also brought considerable media attention to a city-wide problem. Suddenly, the issue of bleak school grounds was in front of administrators and decision-makers; and during the next two years the contest attracted donations of thousands of dollars worth of plants, labor and materials from community organizations. While there is only one winner each year, the contest encourages all schools to take notice of the physical condition of their schoolyards and reflect on the extent to which they offer an educational and life-enhancing environment for children.

For school boards and organizations advocating greener schoolyards, an Ugliest School Yard Contest offers a way to rally resources for school grounds projects, providing an especial benefit to schools in poorer neighborhoods where fundraising may be a barrier. It's a sure bet that there will be no shortage of well-qualified entrants. When *Green Teacher* magazine posted a notice on the worldwide web in 1998 asking if anyone had ever heard of an ugliest schoolyard contest, the response was overwhelming — not because anyone actually knew of such a contest, but because everyone had a school to nominate, including one respondent who wanted to nominate every public school in New York City.

Top: St. Anthony School's winning schoolyard. Below: The project after one growing season: trees are planted in mounded groves and paths direct foot traffic away from their root zones.

Whether you live in New York City or Nakusp, here are some basic guidelines for organizing an Ugliest School Yard Contest.

Set a timeline
Ensure that the schedule allows plenty of time for recruiting key volunteers and sponsors.

Time to deadline	Task
12 months	Form a contest committee of interested individuals.
10 months	Recruit one or more sponsors willing to donate a cash prize.
8 months	Recruit an organization or individual with expertise to help the winning school design and implement their greening project.
6 months	Form a judging panel of up to six members selected from the contest committee and contest sponsors. Set a date for judging the entries.
3 months	Send entry forms and contest rules to schools.

Prepare entry forms

Schools should submit:

- a written description of their school grounds with photos showing several views

- a site plan of the area to be "greened"

- letters of support from the principal and parent council

- a proposal outlining how the prize money will be put to use

- information on the number of students in the school; the size of the grounds; the percentage covered by buildings, grass and asphalt; the amount of shade and seating available; and the existing vegetation

Pick a winner

Select the winner based not just on the bleakness of the schoolyard, but on the quality of the proposal and the evidence of leadership and commitment to transforming the schoolyard. If the judges cannot agree on the ugliest entry, visit the schools and meet the principals.

Publicize the winning school at a special presentation in the schoolyard. Invite local politicians and media to attend. In press releases, encourage the donation of funds, materials and labor by individuals and businesses in the community. ✎

Tim Grant and Gail Littlejohn are the editors of Green Teacher *magazine.*

Thanks to Ann Coffey for her suggestions. For more information, contact: School Grounds Transformation Programme, Canadian Biodiversity Institute, S-322, 99 Fifth Avenue, Ottawa, ON, K1S 5P5, (613) 235-7550, e-mail harbour@magma.ca.

Top: Students setting up composters. Bottom: Colorful snakes serve as both pavement games and winding paths that lead to the entrance of the nature area.

A Step-by-step Planning Guide

The installation of a naturalized area on the school grounds provides many opportunities for participants of different levels of ability. Planning ahead and developing a checklist of tasks will keep things in order and keep everyone busy. The following steps can be used as a framework for a schoolyard naturalization project.

1. Getting started

❧ Identify reasons for the project. Along with being a teaching tool and a cost-effective outdoor center in the schoolyard, a naturalized area can provide habitat for wildlife, facilitate outdoor maintenance, or screen an undesirable view.

❧ Form a steering committee consisting of a few people with a common goal and lots of energy to get the project wheels turning. Include parents, teachers, student representatives, the school grounds caretaker, and a school administrator.

by Miriam Mutton and Debbie Smith

❧ Establish a philosophy or mandate to clarify your goal and help keep program objectives in line and attainable. A logo or motto gives the project a recognizable identity in the school and community. This visibility is helpful when seeking donations of labor, funds, or materials.

❧ Establish a regular meeting schedule to keep the lines of communication open and clear. Let the frequency of meetings be determined by the stage of project development.

❧ Set up a system to maintain communication within the group, school, and community. Newsletters sent home with students and a letter sent to neighbors will keep parents and local residents informed. Other avenues of communication include the public relations person at the board office and the local media.

Keep everyone busy by assigning work crews to specific tasks.

2. Taking stock of resources

Identify the key roles of the people involved in the project. In most projects, these will include the following groups.

Steering Committee, which will:
❧ initiate the project
❧ establish a need or wish list for the project
❧ raise funds
❧ oversee the project from start to finish
❧ create a watch group to ensure continued care of the project

Project Advisor, a landscape architect, gardening or environmental expert who:
❧ can advise on design and prepares instructions for the installation and care of the project

- may be retained by the steering committee to advise on contracts or agreements with hired help
- can invite a variety of experts to speak to students, share ideas, and critique student designs

Installation Crews, student and community volunteers who will carry out various tasks such as preparing beds, planting, and constructing walkways. For work requiring heavy machinery or the building of structures, the installation crew may include a landscape contractor.

Maintenance Crew, a mixed group with interchangeable members who will water and care for plants over the first two growing seasons while they are getting established. The crew may include custodians, local service groups, students and municipal employees.

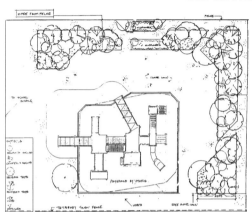

The ultimate aim is to have a self-sustaining and ecologically balanced plant community that is integrated into the local environment.

Volunteers, including members of the steering committee, installation and maintenance crews, and others who will help in planning and implementing the project. Try to be as specific as you can when making requests. A list of tasks to be done helps keep you organized.

Donors, the individuals, organizations and businesses who contribute money, materials or expertise to the project. Generally there is a better chance of obtaining donations if you keep your search local. Spread the news of your project and be prepared when asking for donations: have a good idea of your project plans and be specific in your request.

If looking for donations of labor or expertise, contact the local horticultural society or garden club, environmental groups, young naturalists, outdoor education center, and other community associations. If seeking material goods, draw up a wish list which might include a tree, a shrub, lumber, composted manure, the use of heavy machinery and so forth. In seeking funding, it will help if contributors can associate something tangible with their donation such as a bench or tree or plaque. It can be more difficult to obtain funding for intangibles such as operating costs and rentals. Try to have a few major fundraising events rather than many small ones. Local environment clubs and colleges that offer related programs will have advice about sources of funds.

3. Selecting the site

A good location is an accessible one. Select a site that will not interfere with playing fields, future building expansion, or utility and road upgrading. A new project may also be situated so that it provides a wildlife corridor between existing natural areas. If space on the schoolyard is limited, it may be possible to locate the project on nearby municipal lands. Some municipalities have joint-use agreements to share facilities and maintenance with local school boards. For example, adopt-a-park programs in which a school is granted guardianship of a park have been successfully implemented in some areas.

4. Putting the project in perspective

Identify factors that might influence your project. To help determine the plant community suitable for the site, take an inventory of current conditions. Is the ground low and wet or sloped and dry? Sunny or shady? Are there underground utilities or overhead wires? Neighboring land uses? What are the needs of other users including people and wildlife? Is there a source of water nearby? In what planting zone is the project located?

5. Preparing the plan

The plan, consisting of a site map and plant list, is an important part of the project since it directs future work. The plan may be prepared by a professional landscape designer or a team of knowledgeable persons and interested volunteers, including students. If the project and the research is part of the school curriculum, students can take the lead in preparing the plan.

A plan should include an overhead map of the planting area drawn to a common working scale and having north approximately located. Locate any existing features to be retained or removed. Draw new project ideas, including planting areas, bed edging, paths, and other elements such as benches, signs, and lights. It also is a good idea to determine a water source that can be used during planting and subsequent maintenance and, if lighting is an option, the source of electricity.

The plant list identifies plants by both common and botanical names and has separate categories for shrubs, trees, and wildflowers. In selecting plants for a schoolyard, consideration should be given to the toxicity of plants: parts of some plants, both native and non-native, can be harmful to children if touched or ingested.

6. Installing the project

Implementation of the plan may take place all at once or over several phases. Setting a deadline such as an opening ceremony and working backwards from it is a good way to establish a schedule that allots sufficient time for each phase of the project.

Installation day, when everyone is together on the site, is an exciting time. Careful planning will ensure that work proceeds smoothly. A project coordinator, someone who is well informed of the tasks to be accomplished, should oversee installation and offer practical advice. Organizing students, staff, and other volunteers into installation crews will ensure that everyone has a specific task and that there are enough workers for each job.

In creating a timetable and organizing volunteers, be sure that each part of the project is covered. The following are common aspects of school grounds projects.

Planting techniques should be demonstrated and the site plan clearly mapped.

Layout of bedding edges: Delineate outside edges of the work area and install temporary fencing, such as snow fencing, to remain until completion of work by heavy machinery. Identify and clearly mark the traffic route for vehicles travelling near the playground.

Prepare beds, install perimeter edging: Regrade edges of beds if necessary to ensure drainage. Till the soil to break up grassy cover and reduce compaction. Incorporate a good soil amendment such as well rotted manure or compost to improve soil texture and nutritive qualities. A soil test helps identify deficiencies and may be available from provincial or state agricultural departments.

Plant trees and shrubs: Planting techniques should be demonstrated by the project advisor or other expert. Plants will set down roots before significant top growth begins and this could require two full growing seasons. Regular watering to thoroughly soak the root area is important during this time.

Plant flowers for a wildflower or butterfly garden: Seeds of wildflowers may be started indoors as a classroom project and transplanted outdoors in the spring. In designing a wildflower garden, consider the different life cycles of annuals, biennials, and perennials.

Mulch: A thick layer of mulch over root areas can help conserve moisture while improving soil quality. Soft, aged, dark-colored mulch is best. Shredded wood mulch may be available at minimal cost from local municipalities or landscape companies, but be sure to find out the origin of the material, as roadside shreddings may contain poison ivy. Avoid whole leaves which can mat and suffocate young plants. Instead, combine shredded leaves with wood chips.

Pathways and hard surfaces: As the planting area can be quite a hub of activity on planting day, pathways should be installed either before or after planting. Their surfaces should be porous to permit moisture to soak into the ground below. Hard surfaces that allow drainage include interlocking pavers or a packed surface of fine granular material; soft-surface pathways include grass and wood chips.

Miriam Mutton

Installation day, when all of the groups involved in the project are together on the site, is an exciting time. Careful planning will ensure that work proceeds smoothly.

Grass areas: Surrounding areas of lawn may suffer soil compaction due to heavy traffic during installation and should be aerated and top-dressed to ensure healthier growth. Aeration involves using a machine to remove plugs of soil, which helps to reduce stressful growing conditions resulting from soil compaction. The machine may be available from the school maintenance department or from an equipment rental shop. Top dressing is a technique of lightly raking a combination of seed and light topsoil or compost into the existing grass to thicken growth or to fill in bare patches. The seed mixture should have a high legume content such as white or strawberry clover: legumes fix nitrogen in the soil for use by plants and their flowers provide food for insects. To conserve moisture and promote healthy growing conditions, allow lawn grass to grow higher during summer heat.

7. Recognizing contributors

Keep notes of all those who have contributed their time, funds, materials or advice to the project. A thank-you card or an invitation to an official opening brings everyone together. Small tokens of thanks, such as plaques or bricks, are well appreciated by all. Public acknowledgement is important.

8. Arranging ongoing care of the project

Maintenance, particularly watering during the summer, is essential to the establishment of new plants. As the plants mature, some pruning may also be necessary. Parents, student volunteers, and maintenance staff will need to help during these formative years. A diary of notes and photographs is a good way to document progress in the naturalized area and serves as a keepsake.

As the outdoor classroom matures, its progress will become a focal point for study and a source of enjoyment. The ultimate aim, after initial nurturing, is to have a self-sustaining and ecologically balanced plant community that is integrated into the local environment, as well as into the everyday life of the school and surrounding community. &

Debbie Smith is a primary teacher at Burnham School in Cobourg, Ontario, who acted as teacher liaison on the school's outdoor classroom project. Miriam Mutton is a landscape architect in Cobourg, Ontario, who has assisted in the design and installation of several school grounds projects.

School Grounds in a Box: Model-making and Design

Thinking of transforming your school grounds but having trouble knowing where to start? Feeling intimidated by the site plan? Then why not try making a large model?

Most people are visual learners and have trouble translating a two-dimensional site plan into a three-dimensional space and vice versa. Making a large, three-dimensional model of your school grounds will enable you to visualize the project as you develop a plan for the site. A model will also make it easy to explore and evaluate the various options you are considering. By making movable to-scale replicas of components such as fences, pathways, and plantings, you can determine the best placement of the various elements you have in mind, avoiding pitfalls such as placing conflicting activities side by side, obstructing sight lines, and locating projects across "desire lines" (non-designated pathways that people choose to use to get from one place to another).

by Ann Coffey

A model can be invaluable in generating excitement for the project among the school community, in gaining the support of school board planners, and in raising funds. Integrating model-making into the curriculum intimately connects children with every part of their school grounds and helps generate a sense of ownership in the project. Students of all ages love building the various components and experimenting with locating them in different places. And through this engaging, creative play, all participants in a project are able to share their ideas and visually consider how to adapt these ideas to the conditions, constraints and uses of the site.

A 10' x 12' model with to-scale mock-ups of proposed projects.

Ann Coffey

Gathering data

The first step in creating a model is to determine the "as is" characteristics of your school grounds. This includes checking the accuracy of dimensions on the school's site plan and surveying the present conditions, features, and uses of the grounds.

A site survey is conducted to identify and measure existing features such as vegetation, fences, and playing fields; to assess site conditions such as drainage, wind patterns, graffiti, and litter; and to determine the various uses of the grounds by school and community. It is helpful to record this information directly on the school's site plan (usually obtainable from the school board).

A biodiversity inventory, ideally conducted over the course of a year, identifies the plants and wildlife that already inhabit or visit the site. Students can make a biodiversity map showing where and when the species identified were found and then use this information as baseline data for monitoring changes in biodiversity through subsequent years.

A shade audit helps in determining where additional shade is needed on the grounds. The areas of shade should be measured early in the morning, at noon, and at the end of the day at intervals throughout the year. Repeating the audit annually will enable you to monitor the increase in shade over time as the result of planting trees, growing vines on fences, and constructing shelters such as gazebos.

Involving students in surveying the site is a good way to begin to integrate school grounds transformation into the curriculum. For example, students can record and compare data, observe seasonal changes, identify plants and animals, measure buildings and fences, estimate the height of trees, calculate the area of the grounds covered by buildings, paving, grass and natural spaces, and measure the area of shade cast by buildings and trees at different times of the day throughout the year. The greater students' involvement during this initial planning stage, the greater their sense of ownership as the project evolves.

Building the model
Determining scale

A school grounds model need not be as precise as the site plan; however, keep in mind that details on the three-dimensional model will eventually need to be transferred to the two-dimensional site plan for presentation to the school board. The transfer of data will be simpler if the dimensions of the various components of the model are as accurate as possible and on a scale that is easy to work with. For example, if the site plan measures 2' x 2' 6" and the model is made exactly five times larger (10' x 12' 6"), measurements taken from the site plan will be multiplied by five and those from the model will be divided by five.

Assembling materials

Once you have surveyed and measured the components of the site, the model can be made easily and cheaply using scrap and "found" materials. The following are suggestions for representing the existing features and surfaces of the grounds and for building to-scale maquettes (small models, mock-ups, or three-dimensional sketches) of proposed projects:

Before: A bare "as is" model of the school building, pavement and playing field. After: With plantings, play structures and pavement games in place, it is easy to check sight lines, shade patterns and the compatibility of adjacent activities.

❧ Cut cardboard boxes to size to form the buildings. Draw doorways and windows and mark spaces where murals can be added.

❧ Use gray fabric or carpeting to represent paved areas such as playgrounds, pathways, parking lots, and fire lanes.

❧ Paint existing pavement games such as hopscotch and four square directly onto the gray fabric. If plans involve removing, relocating or adding games such as a chess board or number snakes, paint them on separate scraps of fabric so they can be tried out in different locations.

❧ Use green fabric or carpeting for sports fields and other grassed spaces. Indicate bare patches with earth-colored material.

❧ Make fences by drilling holes in lengths of 1" x 2" lumber and gluing short sections of dowel into the holes. Attach wire mesh to the fence posts to represent chain-link fences. Ensure that the distance between posts and the height of the fencing is scaled in accordance with measurements taken during the site survey.

❧ Make models of trees and other plants using dead or unwanted branches from trees and shrubs and setting them in a base of plaster or plasticene.

❧ Lay colored string on the grounds of the model to mark routes used by pedestrians and cyclists. Use string of a contrasting color to mark routes for vehicles.

Getting Started

Model-builders can have fun using their imagination to add foliage to vegetation and to make miniature play structures, basketball poles, bike racks, storage sheds, dumpsters, and seating.

Marking the grounds of the model

To identify the best areas for your projects, it is useful to transfer the following information from your site surveys to the model:

❧ utilities infrastructure and the area around each installation that must remain accessible for repair and maintenance work

❧ areas where snow is piled in winter

❧ access routes and turning-space allowances for maintenance, emergency, delivery, and waste-collection vehicles

❧ routes used by pedestrians and cyclists to enter and exit the grounds and buildings, and routes between the building and various destinations on the grounds such as play structures, sports fields, bike racks, dumpsters, storage sheds, portable classrooms, outdoor seating, parking spaces, and bus stops

❧ problem areas such as poor drainage, steep slopes, diseased trees, windy spots, places where litter collects, undesirable site uses, graffiti, and damaged fences and signs

❧ off-limits areas

❧ sight lines that must be retained for supervision

❧ wildlife observed on the site, both seasonally and year-round

❧ various uses of the grounds by the school and community, as well as comments by students, parents or teachers

Write short notes and comments on paper and attach them directly to the model or mark important spots with numbers or letters and make an annotated key. Take photographs of unsightly views that you wish to improve upon as well as the more attractive views you would like to preserve. Place them within the model or around the property boundaries to serve as a reminder.

Green fences: Cedar cuttings model a natural screen along a fenceline; grapevines transform a chain-link fence with seasonal greenery and food for birds.

Ann Coffey

Ann Coffey

Redesigning the grounds

Once the model of the existing site has been constructed, add to-scale maquettes of proposed projects. Determine the best location for new projects by placing them within the grounds of the model and checking to make sure that:

❧ projects are not placed across "desire lines"

❧ shade from trees will fall where it is needed

❧ sight lines from the street, from important vantage points across the yard, and from the building are not obstructed

❧ incompatible activities and uses are not placed side by side (children playing on a paved basketball court can slip and hurt themselves on pea gravel kicked from under an adjacent swing set)

Vegetation

In addition to constructing to-scale models of existing trees and shrubs, make models of proposed trees to show the height and spread at the time of planting as well as the size they are expected to attain at maturity. Positioning these trees in different locations on the model will help you decide where to plant them and ensure that sufficient space is allotted for growth.

Knowing how people and vehicles traverse the site helps to avoid problems that may arise from planting trees, shrubs and gardens on "desire lines" or in areas where vegetation may suffer mechanical damage from vehicles. If it is not possible to avoid planting across a well-used route, anticipate that people will tend to walk across the new planting rather than around it and design a clearly-marked pathway to guide them through the space. Create pathways that are interesting to follow: for example, use stepping stones, concrete shapes with animal paw prints, or boards with carvings of words or symbols.

Seating

Place maquettes of various types of seating in different configurations on the model. Remember that children are much more interested in having pleasant places to sit *in* than simply nice things to sit *on*. Design seating arrangements according to the play activities that children engage in and consider installing enough seating to accommodate an entire class during outdoor studies.

Ann Coffey

A model provides a focal point during information sessions with parents and community members.

Sight lines

Safety is one of the main concerns of school boards, parents and neighbors. To ensure that your design does not compromise visual supervision of the grounds, check that new projects do not obstruct important sight lines. You can do this easily by lying down on the ground to get a worm's eye view from different points on the model.

Shade

Once you have positioned the maquettes of trees, gazebos and other projects on the grounds of the model, move spotlights across the model from east to west to simulate the sun's path throughout the day to ensure that shade will fall where it is needed.

Displaying and storing the model

Find a space in the school where the model can remain set up while it is being built. It can be used for class discussions and information sessions with parent and community groups. As the potential for greening the grounds becomes visible, the model will generate and maintain excitement which will help to keep work on the project moving ahead. Where space is limited, photographs of the model can be displayed instead.

Although a model takes up a lot of floor space, you can easily roll up the fabric or carpet base and store it in a box along with the maquettes of your proposed projects. This makes it easy to transport the model should you need to display it off-site when seeking approval or funding for your project.

School grounds design checklist

Check the following to make sure that you are redesigning the grounds according to site conditions and the needs of the school community.

❑ **Division of space:** Does your plan reflect the play and social needs of children, and have you divided the space equitably between grade levels?

❑ **Reducing congestion:** Have you considered how congestion around play equipment can be reduced by increasing the appeal of open spaces that are currently little used or by designing a trail of activities to give more children more play opportunities?

❑ **Scale:** Have you observed children at play and planned to create spaces that are child-scale to increase the sense of comfort and security?

❑ **Sense of place:** Have you created spaces that help develop in children a sense of attachment to a place? These are places where children can learn about nature on their own by observing, listening, smelling, touching, watching bugs, exploring the soil, collecting plant debris, finding feathers, etc.

❑ **Variety:** Are you making the grounds more interesting and providing children with a range of play, social, and learning opportunities?

❑ **Compatibility:** Have you ensured that adjacent play or social spaces are compatible with one another? How will new or existing activities affect new or existing planted areas?

❑ **Comfort:** Have you considered how to make the schoolyard more comfortable by creating windbreaks, shade, and quiet spaces where children can get away from noisy, boisterous play?

❑ **Siblings and friends:** If your yard is segregated by grade, have you considered creating special meeting places where siblings and friends in different grades can play and socialize together?

❑ **Visual appeal:** Have you included ways to make the schoolyard more colorful year round by adding murals, pavement paintings, etc.?

❑ **Fences:** How have you addressed the need to reduce the prison-like aspect of metal fencing? Have you planned to green up fencing or to plant vegetation to screen unsightly views from the schoolyard?

❑ **Wildlife:** Have you ensured that wildlife habitat projects are not placed next to active sports areas where they can be damaged by stray balls and children running?

❑ **Seating:** Have you placed seating out of the way of ball games and other activities? Are the shapes and arrangements of seats appropriate for their uses by children?

❑ **Paving:** Have you ensured that loose materials such as sand, wood chips, and gravel in play spaces and plantings will not spill over onto paved areas and cause children to slip and fall?

❑ **Garbage:** Have you planned to reduce lunchtime garbage and regularly pick up litter that blows into the yard?

❑ **Vandalism:** Have you planned how you will respond to vandalism of your projects?

❑ **Drainage:** Have you assessed how the flow of rainwater or meltwater will be affected by new projects? Have you planned to include shallow swales to interrupt the flow of water and direct it towards rather than away from new plantings?

❑ **All seasons:** Have you visualized what your school grounds will look like during the winter months and how your greening projects will be both used and protected? Have you included winter habitat for wildlife? ❧

Have you visualized what your school grounds will look like during the winter months and how your greening projects will be both used and protected? Have you included winter habitat for wildlife?

Ann Coffey is the Coordinator of the School Grounds Transformation Programme at the Canadian Biodiversity Institute in Ottawa, Ontario. School Grounds in a Box is a trademarked program of the institute.

Greening High Schools: Leaping Subject Barriers

hile many elementary schools have successfully developed school gardens and nature areas, such projects have been quite challenging for high schools. The subject-based curricula and rigid timetables of high schools are formidable barriers to initiating a project as a school-wide endeavor, and most projects are too large an undertaking for one department. But all is not bleak. In fact, high schools have some advantages when it comes to schoolyard greening projects:

by Barbara Kerby and John Egana

↝ High school campuses are typically much larger than the grounds of elementary schools. Consequently, finding a site for a nature area or outdoor classroom may be easier. High schools are also likely to have courtyards and other areas near the school building that are unused. Similarly, schools often have safety zones around ball fields that must be maintained but are not used during the school day.

↝ Many school districts have service learning programs through which high school students receive academic credit for performing community service. Ecological restoration projects in schoolyards and in the surrounding community offer tremendous rewards as service learning projects. (Check to ensure that your school's rules allow community service hours to be applied to a school grounds project.)

↝ Being more mature and physically stronger than elementary students, high school students are capable of undertaking a much greater proportion of the planning, fundraising and installation of school grounds projects.

↝ The budgets of high schools are usually larger than those of elementary schools and thus there is greater potential to support school ground greening projects. If several subject departments are involved, each can provide some funds without straining their individual budgets. If large numbers of students are involved, the administration may support the project with money from the school's discretionary fund. Most important, however, high school students themselves are capable of writing proposals for grants and raising funds in their communities.

An unused area behind a stadium is the site of a restoration project at Lely High School, Naples, Florida.

John Egana

Involving multiple departments

It is usually the science department which initiates an environmental project, but there are many roles for other teachers and departments. In fact, school grounds naturalization is a perfect project for integrating learning in a number of subject areas while still retaining the subject focus. For example, the art department could help design the layout of the garden and use the naturalized area for drawing classes.

The media department could document the project for the school television station, newspaper or yearbook. Economics classes could be directly involved in budgeting and management, and could use the project as a case study in how funding, needs and aesthetics affect decision-making. The math department could tabulate soil or water test results and keep the databases. Convincing departments to get involved is easier than it seems. Classes in subjects like mathematics that do not usually enjoy field trips may be thrilled to spend a class period on the school grounds. With no permission slips required or extra costs for buses, only the time has to be budgeted.

A project undertaken at Lely High School in Naples, Florida, offers an excellent example of the way in which several departments can participate in a school grounds project. At Lely, the original idea was a modest one, to create a cross-country practice trail around a storm water pond located behind a football stadium. However, the track coach, also a science teacher, realized this was a perfect opportunity for the environmental, biology and marine biology classes to get involved in a hands-on restoration project. Students removed invasive plants around the edge of the pond, refurbished an unused rooftop greenhouse, and propagated native plants from cuttings and transplants. They learned mapping and GPS (global positioning system) skills in order to create the new habitat areas, and began keeping a database to determine whether the native plants are effective in creating habitat areas for wildlife. To enhance the naturalized area, they stocked the pond with fish and planted a privacy hedge between it and the adjoining subdivision.

John Egana

Any project with gardens will need a place for growing plants. At Lely High School an unused rooftop greenhouse was refurbished as a student project. Heavy clear plastic panels cover a basic framework and rough wooden tables provide the work area. A simple greenhouse of this type could be erected in any unused sunny area on the school grounds.

The science teachers recruited the vocational/technical department to design and build a dock from which to perform water quality tests at the pond, as well as outdoor tables for use in experiments. Students now regularly test the pond water and add the results to a database of water quality information. The school maintenance department uses the water quality data to track runoff from fertilizer used on the athletic field. The pond is part of the school storm water management system, and keeping it clear of trash and invasive plants has helped to reduce the risk of flooding on the school grounds.

To promote problem-solving skills, language arts teachers incorporated logistical and planning issues related to the project into a unit on critical thinking. They now lead their classes on trail walks to establish shared experiences that later become the basis of expository writing and stories. In the instructional technology and desktop publishing classes, students have published the ongoing story of the project, along with digital images, on the school web site and in the newsletter.

Student interest has remained high. Having started with a butterfly garden, they are now creating other specialty gardens for students and citizens to enjoy. Each year, roughly 700 students (one-third of the student body) at Lely have hands-on experience with the project. It grows and changes over time as each class contributes to the existing databases and introduces new ideas.

Extra-curricular opportunities

There is little doubt that the schedules of most high schools make it difficult for students to spend significant amounts of time outside each day during their regular classes. However, extra-curricular clubs can also support school grounds greening projects. For example, a school's Envirothon team could use the project to hone their environmental study skills to prepare for regional and international Envirothon competitions.[1] The environmental focus of agricultural clubs such as 4-H or Future Farmers of America would also support participation in these projects. An environment club could become involved in one of the many environmental monitoring programs sponsored by government agencies. For example, the GLOBE project is an international program through which students perform specific environmental experiments in their schoolyards and post the results on a web site[2] where they are used by scientists.

Sustaining interest

If students design the project, it is more likely that their interest levels will remain high. At Lely, the science teachers outlined a study plan for the area and encouraged students to contribute ideas for projects such as removing invasive plants, renovating the greenhouse, and creating a water quality database. As each phase of the project was completed, students provided input into its next phase. In addition, the work of developing the pond was linked to science fair projects and other student competitions.

John Egana

The best side-effect of such a project may be in the way it helps students forge an identity as a student body and as individuals.

Students' interest is also sustained by opportunities to link with the wider community. Students can take on the tasks of recruiting outside organizations and businesses to help with the project and inviting guest speakers from the community. This will not only give students access to real-life experts to answer their questions, but also create networking opportunities which may lead to internships, summer or permanent jobs, or further fields of study through working with outside companies.

Another possible motivational activity is for students to compare their school project to a local or national environmental project, such as the restoration of the Everglades here in Florida. Students could follow the national project in the media and through web sites. At the same time, they would document their own project through school and local media and by creating their own web site.

While school grounds projects may be challenging for high schools to undertake, the large number of related academic topics that can be covered makes them worthwhile. But the best side-effect of such a project may be in the way it helps students forge an identity as a student body and as individuals. Through a project involving several school departments as well as local organizations and businesses, students form new bonds and are exposed to career options they may have never considered. And their hands-on participation may give them a feeling of greater self-worth at a time when many young people often feel themselves to be just a faceless part of a large institution.

Barbara Kerby works in public affairs for Big Cypress Basin in Naples, Florida. John Egana teaches at Lely High School, also in Naples.

Notes

[1] Envirothons are annual team competitions which test high school students' knowledge of environmental topics. Teams who win at the state or provincial level go on to compete in North American finals. See the Envirothon web site at www.envirothon.org

[2] See the GLOBE web site at www.globe.fsl.noaa.gov

John Egana

Greening the Grounds

🍃 **A Diverse Dozen: Habitats for Healthy School Grounds** by Paul E. Knoop

🍃 **Rethinking Tree Planting** by Henry Kock

🍃 **Natural Wetlands and Retention Ponds** by Jackie Oblak

🍃 **Bringing Back the Prairie: Ecological Restoration** by Molly Fifield Murray

🍃 **Desert and Dryland Gardens** by Janet Fox

🍃 **Creating a Schoolyard Tree Nursery** by Cathy Dueck

🍃 **Rooftop Gardens** by Monica Kuhn

A Diverse Dozen:
Habitats for Healthy School Grounds

by Paul E. Knoop

For the first time in human history, many children are growing up in biologically impoverished environments. In our cities and suburbs, few of the original landforms, streams, natural ecosystems, or wild plants and animals still exist. Schools can help to fill this void by creating diverse learning environments around school buildings. Here are a few suggestions.

A WET AREA such as a stream, pond, or marshy spot will attract larger animals and provide habitat for turtles, fish, frogs, and salamanders. Natural wetlands are among the richest areas biologically, but are often ignored and too often destroyed.

Boardwalk, bridge, ponds and seating areas at St. Matthew Secret Garden in Regina, Saskatchewan.

A HARDWOOD FOREST should include native hardwood trees: oaks, maples, hickories, walnuts, ashes, cottonwood, and others. Dead and decaying logs, stumps, and leaves should be allowed to remain in the woodland. Other plants, including native shrubs and wildflowers common to wooded areas, will add beauty and diversity.

PINES OR OTHER EVERGREENS provide a completely different habitat. Owls, small songbirds, squirrels, and other interesting animals utilize evergreens. These also provide attractive green in winter and are aesthetically pleasing. Plant evergreens in clusters rather than rows to provide maximum interior cover for wildlife.

A TALL OR SHORT GRASS PRAIRIE consists of native grasses and wildflowers and is a place of great beauty. The prairie landscape is a significant part of our natural and historic heritage. Ethics, land use, and conservation of resources can be taught if this resource is available to students.

A BRUSH PILE OR FENCE ROW can provide the food, cover, and space necessary to attract birds, mammals, and other animals. Fence rows also act as wind breaks and travelways for wild creatures and add color and texture to the landscape.

AN UNMOWED MEADOW OR ISLANDS OF VEGETATION growing in a lawn will harbor an abundance of meadow wildflowers, tall grasses, small mammals, and birds.

A BOULDER FIELD can include large glacial erratics, pieces of sandstone, or flat lime-stone rocks bearing fossils. This adds interest to the site and aids in the study of geology. Smaller rocks will provide habitat for a variety of small creatures: earth-worms, sowbugs, salamanders, centipedes, millipedes and others.

A HILL is useful for giving a different perspective to the school ground, learning mapping skills, and illustrating erosion and other physical laws.

VEGETABLE GARDEN PLOTS offer an opportunity to watch food grow and be harvested. Organic methods and biological control of insects and weeds can be demonstrated.

A COMPOST PILE offers the opportunity to observe natural recy-cling while keeping cafeteria, lawn, and garden scraps from being sent off to the landfill.

AN OUTDOOR SEATING AREA can be incorporated anywhere on school property. Benches, large logs, or log stools that are comfortable and provide off-the-ground seating should accommodate at least 30 students.

FEEDING STATIONS AND NEST BOXES for birds and mammals can be placed in a variety of areas. These, along with plant cover placed close to school windows, offer the best opportunities to observe wildlife.

When making changes in your school site, keep the following points in mind:

⤙ Establish a number of diverse natural communities. Because each habitat sup-ports different plants and animals, many new species will come into newly created areas. Unmowed meadows, woodlots, wet areas and undisturbed edges between habitats encourage diversity of wild plants and animals.

⤙ Give your site time to develop fully. Plantings, wet spots and unmowed areas will not immediately become mature natural communities. Be patient!

⤙ Use native species whenever possible. Native plants are more likely to sur-vive because they are acclimated to the area. Including native plants may also help to preserve rare species whose populations are being reduced by loss of habitat. ❧

Paul E. Knoop is a naturalist and educator in Laurelville, Ohio.

Feeding stations and native plants attract wildlife. Here a blue jay stakes claim to a feeder and a monarch caterpillar makes its way on a milkweed leaf.

Peter Rasberry

Karen Oberhauser

Rethinking Tree Planting

by Henry Kock

The vigorous campaigns and many resources devoted to planting trees in recent years have been well intended. But too often tree planting is promoted as a panacea for much that ails the planet: "Trees take carbon dioxide from the air and help stop global warming," say the experts. "Trees provide habitat and halt species extinction." Millions of tree seed packets and cute little boxes are handed out by "green" businesses across North America. The little boxes contain a seed, a peat pellet, and elaborate instructions. They claim that if you grow the seed and keep it alive, you will "save the Earth." But what if the tree dies or, for that matter, lives, and the Earth remains polluted? What is the message in this way of teaching our children? Planting trees can be a healthy and important part of a child's learning experience, but a much richer experience awaits those who take a more holistic approach to habitat restoration.

A ravine ditch forms a wildlife corridor on school property.

A gentle plea for a meadow

When we think predominantly of trees, we restrict our knowledge of options. Meadows, for example, are as important as forests in creating a sustainable, biologically diverse landscape. They represent an early stage of forest succession, a dynamic vegetation system and habitat. Yet I have seen many meadows completely filled with newly planted trees. Such plantings will produce good utility poles, but their dense cover can reduce biological and genetic diversity. Where do the foxes, hawks, owls, bluebirds, meadowlarks and bobolinks go?

We must get beyond the temptation to plant all open areas full of trees. We can begin by learning to "read" the local landscape. Many local species will seed themselves naturally into a site if we just stop cutting and learn to watch the natural process over time. In schoolyards adjacent to natural areas, stop mowing in a designated section and observe the natural process of succession. Stop mowing another area every three to five years so that students can observe the transformation and take inventory of the progression of events and patterns.

Schoolyards will not be transformed into forests in one year, nor should they be. Often the soil has been stripped or compacted, resulting in a degraded site that is most suitable for early succession or "pioneer" species such as grasses, goldenrod, sumac, ash, aspen, birch and pine. These sites require a few years of repair with organic matter to develop good soil structure and chemistry before they are planted with forest species such as sugar maple, red oak, tulip tree, hemlock or wild ginger. When the site is ready for trees, plant them in small colonies as nature does, or as a shelter belt that will increase and protect habitat options, not reduce them.

With the help of local nature interpreters students can become familiar with the local natural area. Through art, writing, history, nature study, science and geography, they can come to realize that the dynamic ecosystem they are studying is a fragmented piece of what was originally a huge interconnected system of forest, meadow, and prairie covering the entire continent. By studying topographic maps,

teachers and students can recognize where large-scale plantings are needed to bridge the gaps between remnant fragments of forests, meadows, and watersheds. These linear forests function as highways for wildlife. The maps may also help in identifying the need for windbreaks to reduce soil desiccation and erosion.

Selecting native species

In any program to create habitat, the importance of using plant species that are indigenous to a local area cannot be overstated. The native wildlife has evolved with these plants in the landscape. Native plants are those that were found in pre-European North America; indigenous plants are native plants found in the local bioregion. Again, be suspicious of freebie tree seeds. No single species is indigenous everywhere. Pill box seeds such as red pine will not grow well in heavy loam, clay or mountain soils. In Canada, ponderosa pine is native only to the southern interior of British Columbia. Honey locust will not survive northern winters. Norway spruce may be very adaptive, but like the non-native and invasive Norway maple, it produces such heavy shade that few other plants will grow under it. Imagine these species planted all across North America — the project would not pass an environmental impact study!

There was a time when native plants were very hard to obtain, but plant nurseries now offer a greater variety of indigenous plants. If you cannot purchase them, grow some. Children need an opportunity to observe how long it takes for a tree to grow from seed. During a September walk in a nearby natural area, gather seeds on or under an indigenous tree and plant them in an outdoor seed bed (not in the classroom far removed from natural systems). Students will know where to transplant the seedlings later because they will have become familiar with the community of the parent plant and its soil and moisture requirements.

Caring for trees from the ground up

A holistic approach to habitat restoration enriches the potential for learning about trees and their life support system. The trees, too, may live longer. When people go out to plant thousands of trees on pre-arranged dates in all kinds of weather conditions, it is a triumph of quantity over quality. Even with good follow-up, tree losses can be very high, especially for deciduous species.

The same is true of schoolyard plantings in which trees are often isolated and lack an understory, and thus have no protection for their root zones. Many people imagine that a tree's roots grow straight down, but most roots are actually located within the top 20 cm (8") of soil. The daily parade of tiny footsteps around a schoolyard tree packs the soil and suffocates the roots by reducing air circulation into and out of the soil.

Planting trees can be a healthy and important part of a child's learning experience, but a much richer experience awaits those who take a more holistic approach to habitat restoration.

When, as in natural settings, an understory is left to grow around the tree, the root zone is protected from soil compaction and the tree's roots are properly aerated. An understory not only improves the soil structure, but also enhances its ability to retain and recycle nutrients. When fallen leaves are held in place by understory plants instead of being raked or blown away, their decomposition produces a healthy soil and their nutrients are recycled back to the plants through myriad soil organisms.

Planting trees can be an important part of a child's learning experience. But trees are only one component of a life zone that includes understory plants, ground cover, soil life, and myriad insects, birds and mammals. Restoration is a process that requires the careful observation and interpretation of the dynamic relationships among *all* of these inhabitants. It is a way of working in "consultation" with nature that pays close attention to the process and not the end result. Nature is dynamic and teaches us that change is possible. If we are given the opportunity to observe this for ourselves, we may yet develop a vision of a sustainable civilization. ◈

Henry Kock is a horticulturist at The Arboretum at the University of Guelph in Guelph, Ontario.

Henry Kock

Stop the mower! Schoolyard naturalization projects can be as simple as letting local species seed themselves naturally into the site, a living demonstration of the transformative process of succession.

Natural Wetlands and Retention Ponds

 Anyone who has visited a natural wetland or a forest pond in the spring can attest to the amazing diversity of life in such an area. What many do not realize is that these wet areas play an important role in capturing and filtering surface water runoff and in recharging the water table. By retaining precipitation, they enhance the biotic community in the surrounding area and contribute to the development of the soil itself. In contrast, most urban areas, including most school grounds, have been designed to encourage precipitation to run off as quickly as possible. Rather than percolating into the ground where it falls, water from rain and snow melt flows over paved surfaces, through storm sewers, and into local streams and lakes, often carrying surface contaminants and particles of eroded soil. In many areas, surface runoff is the primary cause of water pollution.

by Jackie Oblak

A school grounds greening project provides an opportunity to manage the flow of water on the grounds by directing downspout and surface runoff to a water-retention pond that simulates a natural wetland or forest pond. The difference between this type of pond and a constructed pond is that the wet area is fed solely by precipitation. By its very nature, then, it may have standing water at certain times of the year and be dry at other times. In nature, such seasonal or vernal ponds provide aquatic habitat for the nymph or larval stages of many insects and the tadpole stage of amphibians. A retention pond, therefore, will not only provide soil moisture for plants and soil-dwelling organisms, but may also attract a number of creatures that would not normally be found in an urban environment. Water retained on the property may also be used for watering gardens and plantings, in turn reducing the demand for municipal water.

Jackie oblak

A formerly vexing mud puddle is now a seasonal pond at Parkdale School in Belleville, Ontario. Boulders furnish a class sitting area on the berm to the left.

Site assessment

A site assessment is the best way to determine the feasibility of creating a wetland on your school grounds, as well as its most suitable location and size. Retention of water depends on several factors including the frequency and volume of precipitation, how much of that precipitation can be captured, the permeability of the soil, the level of the water table, and the capacity of the pond.

Locating a wetland at a relatively low elevation may appear logical, but it must be an area to which water flows from other points on the property. Direct observation is the best teacher: if possible, take students outdoors to observe where water flows during rainstorms or periods of heavy snow melt. Later, map the patterns of flow by transferring observations to overlays on the school's site plan (usually available through the school board). Observations should include a number of points:

↝ Are there obvious flow directions during prime snow melt and heavy rainfalls?

↝ Are some areas lower than others, or do some areas already tend to collect water?

↝ Does water leave the property? Where and how?

- Can you actually see the water running, indicating a fairly fast rate of flow, or are you seeing an area filling up as another empties?
- Where do the rooftop downspouts drain? Could this water be redirected to your potential site?

Estimating water volume

A rough estimate of the volume of precipitation that could be captured will give you an idea of how large a pond would be needed for total retention. This is done by measuring the area of the surfaces that will supply runoff and multiplying by the depth of precipitation. (Ten centimeters of fresh, fluffy snow becomes approximately one centimeter of water during snow melt.) Data on precipitation patterns in your area may be obtained from local meteorological services; or students can use rain gauges to track precipitation over time, comparing their daily observations with weather information from newspapers.

Ideally, a retention pond would be large enough to collect most of the water released during peak periods of rainfall or snow melt. However, in regions where rainstorms and sudden snow melts result in large volumes of surface water being available over short periods of time, total retention is not practical because it would require a pond too large and deep for most schoolyards. In addition, it is difficult to predict capacity requirements at any given time because the amount of water a pond can receive depends not only on previous inflow but also on the level of the water table and rate of percolation through the soil. Given this unpredictability, it is always a good idea to have an overflow regardless of the anticipated volume of your pond. Overflows may be surrounding areas that are allowed to be submerged (similar to the flood plains found in nature), or they may be swales that lead the water off to existing ditches or streams. Swales may also be designed to act as retention areas to a lesser degree. Having a shallow grade and encouraging vegetation growth in the swale will reduce the flow and thus allow percolation and sediment settling. The vegetation will help to clean the water by taking up excess nutrients and contaminants.

Visit seasonal ponds to observe what occurs naturally so that you can provide some of the same components in your yard.

Jackie oblak

Wetland and boardwalk at Bill Mason Outdoor Education Centre, Dunrobin, Ontario.

Analyzing soil permeability

An essential step in deciding the feasibility of creating a "natural" wetland is to determine how well your soil will retain water. Core samples, taken from below the depth of the potential retention area, may be analyzed by looking at the color and grain size and applying the "squeeze test." A dark soil with small bits of vegetation, that holds together loosely when squeezed in the hand but crumbles easily, indicates humus. It is a wonderful medium for growing plants, but will not retain the water in a pond for long. Clay soils have a very small grain size, are often gray, and stick together well if squeezed when damp. Sandy soils have a larger grain, are shades of brown, and tend to crumble when squeezed.

A soil that is primarily clay may hold water for long periods of time, whereas a sandy soil may drain within seconds or minutes. If your soil has a high sand content, a natural wetland may not be feasible unless the water table is close to the surface for a large part of the year. Digging a pit, filling it with water, and observing how long the water remains will give a rough indication of the permeability of the soil (the rate at which water moves through it). A liner will help retain water, but the trade-off is that the moisture will not get to the soil to support plants and natural soil development processes.

Site design

There are many considerations in site design: Will it be a large, formally planted area with a pond in the middle, or a small area with informal plantings? Will there be paths or a boardwalk through the area? What types of vegetation will be planted? What limitations may be imposed by school board guidelines and local bylaws? Public consultation is an important component of the process and will often provide alternative points of view that may not have been considered.

If the pond is intended as a habitat as well as a water-retention area, visit seasonal ponds nearby to observe what occurs naturally in these types of wetlands so that you can provide some of the same components in your yard. Note the plants growing around the pond, as these indigenous species are likely well adapted to local conditions. Retention ponds that have standing water year round will require different species of plants than ponds that have dry seasons. Consider succession. Knowing the successional phase that you are trying to mimic will guide in deciding what species to plant and help you understand how the area will develop over a number of years. Also observe the amount of sunlight and shade on the surface of the water. The cooling effect of shade is important in small aquatic habitats because many invertebrates that spend part of their life cycle in ponds are intolerant of high water temperatures. In addition, lowering air temperature through shading and reducing high winds through screening will help to slow the rate of evaporation from the pond and, to a lesser extent, from the surrounding soil. Soil that is covered with vegetation or mulch will generally retain moisture longer.

Do not remove native plants from natural areas. Nursery-grown stock of many native species, including aquatic plants, can be obtained from gardening centers. Alternatively, it may be possible to get permission from landowners to salvage native plants from sites scheduled for development. As for aquatic insects or other creatures, if the new area provides a good habitat for a species, they will find it. Importing creatures is not recommended.

Implementation and celebration

Much of the physical work of marking and digging a pond site can be done by students. The depth will vary from one site to the next, depending on factors such as the volume of water to be retained and limits imposed in local bylaws; but in most cases, it should be possible for students to hand-dig the area using shovels. Supervision at this stage is absolutely necessary to ensure safe use of tools and proper implementation of the design. If the soil that is removed will be used to construct berms or build up garden areas, ensure that participants know where to place it. Document your progress with photographs which can later be used for tracking changes in the wetland over time. When the pond has been dug, the trails have been marked, and the plants are in the ground, make a big deal of it! Celebrate with a grand opening, recognizing all students, staff and volunteers who have contributed.

There are countless ways to modify and adapt the concept of a retention pond. Whether the pond is big or small, and whether it is primarily intended to retain runoff or to provide habitat (or both), capturing precipitation on your school grounds will help to maintain soil moisture and reduce the environmental stress caused by surface runoff streaming into local waterways. Equally important, it is a project that presents unlimited opportunities for multidisciplinary, hands-on learning. Keep in mind that the process is as important as the final product, and creating a retention pond or wetland will be an extraordinary adventure for all involved. ❧

Jackie Oblak is an environmental educator at the Bill Mason Centre of the Ottawa-Carleton District School Board in Ottawa, Ontario.

THIS AREA HAS BEEN DEVELOPED TO RETURN TO A NATURAL STATE FOR THE BENEFIT OF PARKDALE SCHOOL & THE COMMUNITY. TREES, SHRUBS, BIRDS & OTHER WILD LIFE HELP MAKE THIS A UNIQUE CLASSROOM. PLEASE RESPECT & HELP PRESERVE THIS AREA WHILE ENJOYING THE SCHOOL GROUNDS

Jackie oblak

Jackie oblak

Cattails and other wetland plants were salvaged from a building site. Frogs and dragonflies found the new pond within a week.

Bringing Back the Prairie: Ecological Restoration

by Molly Fifield Murray

I n the schoolyard prairie, some children are following butterflies from flower to flower. Others are sketching the intricate landscape. Others have a stopwatch and are recording data as a small experiment unfolds. Amidst drifts of prairie flowers and grasses, some are bending to water and weed the restored prairie that they helped to create.

The great conservationist Aldo Leopold wrote that "When we see land as a community to which we belong, we may begin to use it with love and respect."[1] But in our increasingly urban landscapes, providing opportunities for young people to see and experience the land as a community can be challenging. Students may be instructed that a natural, biotic community is a complex system of living things interacting with soil, water, and climate; but many have little notion of what their own natural community looks like and would have difficulty identifying more than a few of its native members. One way to remedy this, and at the same time to beautify your school grounds and create habitat for wildlife, is to recreate a native ecosystem using the principles of ecological restoration.

A patch of prairie grows relatively quickly, making it a rewarding project for schools.

What is ecological restoration?

Prior to pioneer settlement, North America was home to a rich array of ecosystems, each adapted to the conditions of its particular region. But European settlement brought substantial change to the landscape. Native ecosystems were replaced by acres of corn and wheat and by roads, towns and cities. Waterways were altered and many wetlands drained. Human pressures such as these have led to a decline of native ecosystems and natural biodiversity all over North America.

Ecological restoration grew out of the recognition that biological diversity is essential to the health of the planet and thus to the health of our own species. It is the attempt to replicate a native ecosystem in the region where it once occurred, or where current conditions allow it to occur now. Restoration involves studying a remnant of the original plant community, if one exists, and then replicating it by planting as many species as possible that once grew together. This assemblage of plants will in turn attract the species of insects, mammals and birds that lived there. Restoration may also involve replicating the natural processes that affected that ecosystem, if they are not still naturally present. Participation in ecological restoration promotes responsibility for an ethical relationship with the land. It also offers a way to get in touch with the Native and pioneer relationship to the land in a way that other gardening does not.

Although many ecosystems might be replicated in the schoolyard, prairie restoration offers a number of educational and practical advantages. First, the grasslands of North America once made up the largest contiguous ecosystem on the continent, and the importance of this ecosystem to the settlement and prosperity of the continent is well-documented.[2] A prairie restoration thus affords rich opportunities for studying not only the original ecological relationships but also the social and historical forces that altered the land. Second, the restoration of prairie can happen relatively quickly and in a relatively small area, making it a feasible project for a school. Finally, because some prairie restoration projects have been underway for decades, we now have the benefit of a great deal of research to understand how to proceed.

The restoration process outlined below has been used primarily for prairie restoration, but can be used to restore any ecosystem for which the site is suitable and the plants or seeds available.

A prairie restoration project

Prairies and savannas are described as grasslands because they are dominated, in number of stems, by grasses. But there are hundreds of species of herbaceous non-grasses, called forbs, in the prairies. For instance, in our arboretum's 60-acre prairie restoration, there are over 300 species of plants. About 14 of these species come into bloom each week throughout the growing season, offering a rich array of ever-changing color.

When planning a prairie restoration, the best advice is to start small and go slowly. Keep in mind that the educational value of the restoration comes from involving students in the process as much as in creating the final product. Right from the start, build a coalition of interested people, including school administrators, grounds-maintenance staff, parents, community members and, possibly, a prairie expert to advise on design. Involve students in as many aspects of the planning and implementation of the project as possible. Coordinate with teachers at different grade levels to divide up the curricular opportunities.

Sweet black-eyed Susan: different prairie species come into bloom every week during the growing season.

Research the site

- Research land ownership history
- Interview residents
- Find the original land survey

Researching the site is a great way to integrate social studies and language arts into what would seem to be a science project. Start with aboriginal peoples before European settlement, studying their relationships to the ecosystems present at that time, how they used the prairie and how the prairie sustained them with food and medicines.

Original land surveys can often be obtained from historical societies or public archives, commissioners of public lands or land registry offices. These surveys can provide information about the ecosystems of the 1800s and about patterns of European settlement. In the midwest United States, for instance, the land was laid out in a grid system of one-mile squares without regard to land forms. From census and tax assessment records, local histories and other original sources, students can also learn about the individuals who settled the area. Interviewing older residents or those with a long family history in the area may yield fascinating stories about early days on the prairie.

Plan the site

- Conduct a site analysis
- Locate remnants as models
- Create a design
- Develop a project budget

The planning stage offers great opportunities for hands-on investigations. If possible, locate a model of the ecosystem that you want to replicate, either a fine restoration or a nearby remnant with site characteristics (soil, sun, temperature, precipitation) similar to your own. Studying both the school site and the model ecosystem allows students to investigate the difference in biodiversity between most school grounds and natural areas.

Creating a design takes students through critical thinking: What is necessary to plant to create the visual essence of a prairie? What species mix will attract butterflies and birds? What species mix will provide the widest range of flowering times and represent the plant families of a prairie? What size and shape creates good habitat? Nurseries that sell native plants and seeds often have excellent catalogs containing information on the uses of plants. A useful aid in the planning is to chart a matrix of plants and their characteristics so that you can see how your selections fit your criteria. Ask a local prairie expert or gardener to look over your design when it is complete.

The decision whether to plant seeds, plants, seedlings, or a combination, will be largely determined by your budget. Plants obtained from native plant nurseries will be the most expensive choice, but are the quickest route to a flowering prairie.

It is best to start small — with 1,000 square feet or so — to gain experience with the design, preparation and planting processes. If the entire area is planned from the beginning, successional classes of students can plan for enrichment plantings later.

A prairie restoration affords rich opportunities for studying not only the original ecological relationships but also the social and historical forces that altered the land.

Prepare the site

- Mulch or sod removal
- Remove unwanted species

Site preparation is the single most important factor in the success of a prairie planting. It is very important to identify the weeds on your site so you know the type and extent of preparation you need to do. A site should be prepared in much the same way that a garden or lawn is prepared to receive seeds that will come in contact with the mineral soil. Some people advocate burning the site and throwing the seed onto the burned ground. However, this is an unproven technique and may work best if the plants burned off were primarily bluegrass rather than weeds or other lawn plants.

The soil needs to have good tilth so that the seeds establish root systems when they germinate. If you have a good weed-free lawn on your site, a simple method of preparation is to remove the sod and plant into the loosened soil. You can till the soil if it is hard packed, but tilling may stimulate the germination of weed seeds which you will need to eliminate. The goal in weed removal is to eliminate seeds from annual weeds and to eliminate perennial weeds altogether. If you till the soil, wait at least two weeks after tilling to see what kind of weeds have been stimulated to grow. If they are annuals, mowing them before you plant will prevent them from reseeding. If they are perennials, it is best to eliminate them before planting, using mulches or multiple tilling (for one season or more). We have had success with permeable landscape fabric that smothers plants but allows water into the soil, leaving a fine seed bed after one growing season. Another method of site preparation is to mulch with newspapers covered by wood chips.

You may also want to remove other unwanted species, such as shrubs, particularly non-native shrubs that are aggressive. But even native species such as grey dogwood, aspen and sumac are threats to a prairie planting. These are the pioneers of the forests whose job it is to invade the prairie, modify the environment, and allow forest to grow.

Plant the site

- Collect seed and grow transplants
- Create a planting celebration

Seed collection in the fall is one of the annual rituals of prairie restoration and a wonderful way to introduce students to the ecosystem. Think of beautiful autumn days, warm sun, the smell of prairie grasses, and geese flying overhead.

Molly Murray

If you cannot collect the seed, obtain it from a local native plant nursery, government agency or nature center. Beware of packaged "wildflower mix" which often contains seeds of plants that are not native and may be from distant sources. It is best to deal with a local source in order to obtain seeds from plants growing in climate and soil conditions similar to those at your site.

The seed needs to be in cold storage over winter to mimic winter conditions. In late winter or early spring, students can plant some of the seeds in flats to become familiar with the form of each species at different life stages. They can also create a seedling herbarium to help other students recognize seedlings. This will be a useful reference later when students are weeding a planting.

A spring planting celebration culminates the year's activities and study of the prairie. One part of the celebration at many schools is to have students dance the seeds into the soil. This can be any kind of dance or game that is appropriate to the curriculum you are using. But be sure to remind the students that the goals are to spread the seed evenly over the site, and then to get it in firm contact with the soil. A good way to ensure even spreading of the seed is to line up the entire planting group along one side of the site. Mix the seed with dampened sawdust or vermiculite to give it more volume and make it easier to see where you have planted. Parcel out half of the mixture to the students and challenge them to get across the site with their portion. Then line them up at a 90-degree angle to the planting they just did, and plant the other half of the seed.

Manage the site

- Monitor weeds
- Burn parts of project

Especially during the first year of a prairie planting, it is important to watch for weed growth. Weeds will seldom destroy a prairie planting, but they can slow it down. If a weed problem is really severe you can lose many of your first-germinating prairie species. After planting, monitor the site and be prepared to mow off weeds just as they are flowering. You may need to mow two or three times the first

Keep in mind that the educational value of the restoration comes from involving students in the process as much as in creating the final product.

year, removing the mowed material each time. To avoid lopping off the prairie plants, mow at a height of six inches or more. Most prairie plants are perennials which spend much time establishing deep root systems and do not grow tall the first year, whereas most annual weed species will reach their full height. Do not mow the prairie after the first two years unless you are mimicking grazing or replacing fire as a management tool.

After the second year, there should be enough dead stems to allow you to burn the prairie. Fire was the natural process that maintained native prairies. Burning removes the standing dead vegetation and the heavy layer of dead stems that accumulate and act as a mulch. It also blackens the soil and inhibits woody plants or non-native species which are not adapted to fire. Studies have shown that fire is essential to the health of prairies and increases the flowering of many species, but the optimum frequency and timing of burning is still subject to study. The rule of thumb is to burn only part of a prairie each year so that invertebrates can take refuge in the unburned portion. If burning is not possible, mow and remove the dead vegetation.

Molly Murray

Students dance the seeds into the soil at a spring planting celebration.

Outreach

It is very important to let the larger community know what a prairie is and why it is being planted at school. Otherwise, many people will think it is a patch of weeds that should be sprayed or cut. Using what they have learned about prairies, students can decide on many different ways to inform the community, from making interpretive signs to writing newspaper articles. It is a chance for students to show leadership and develop communication skills in the service of a project that they will care very much about.

The process of changing an ecosystem takes time, as does the process of changing a school's curriculum. Each takes root slowly, but bears rich fruits. ❧

Molly Fifield Murray is Education Manager at the University of Wisconsin-Madison Arboretum in Madison, Wisconsin.

Notes

[1] Aldo Leopold, *A Sand County Almanac* (New York: Oxford University Press, 1949).

[2] See John Madson's *Tallgrass Prairie: A Nature Conservancy Book* (Helena, Montana: Falcon Press, 1993) and *Where the Sky Began: Land of the Tallgrass Prairie* (San Francisco: Sierra Club Books, 1982), and David Costello's *The Prairie World* (New York: Thomas Y. Crowell, 1969).

Desert and Dryland Gardens

The term "desert" may bring to mind a hot, arid, barren wasteland — not the kind of environment that seems conducive to gardening. But, in fact, deserts are fascinating and complex ecosystems that can be replicated as "dryland" gardens in almost any environment. As an outdoor classroom, the desert or dryland garden can give students a unique perspective on water use, plant adaptations in poor soils, and creatures that thrive in hot and dry places.

In creating a desert garden it helps to understand dryland culture. Deserts are not confined to the warmer climates of the world; one-third of the Earth's surface is semi-arid to arid. The common characteristics of drylands include low rainfall (less than 50 cm or 20" of rain per year; less than 25 cm or 10" in true deserts), mean annual temperatures ranging from 2°C to 27°C (35°F to 80°F), and poor, sandy or rocky soils that are free-draining. Deserts or drylands are subject to high winds and periodic downpours, and prone to sudden and rapid erosion. To cope with these extremes, vegetation is typically sparse and low growing, adapted to either escape (annual seeds that lie dormant and await favorable conditions) or survive (plants that conserve water). Given the drought conditions experienced in many temperate areas in recent years, and the poor maintenance school gardens receive during the off-season, plants suited to desert conditions are ideal for school gardens.

by Janet Fox

Janet Fox

Location of your desert garden

Recreating the desert environment in an educational garden bed requires an area that is separate from other gardens. Avoid situating your dry bed in a low spot where water collects. The nice thing about desert gardens is that they can be large or small, depending on your location, budget and needs; even a series of pots can replicate the desert environment.

In more northerly climates an area with good light protected from cold wind is helpful; a southern exposure backed against a wall or building is ideal. In areas that freeze, choosing the right plants and mulching will help avoid loss. In truly cold regions and in areas of very high rainfall and low sunlight your best bet may be container gardening. For those in southern regions with hot dry summers and warm winters, some shade is tolerable, but the garden should receive at least six hours of sunlight daily.

Deserts are fascinating and complex ecosystems that can be replicated as "dryland" gardens in almost any environment.

Soil and water

The right soil conditions are crucial to survival of low-water-use plants. Good drainage is a must. Many experts suggest that it is easier to achieve proper drainage by building raised beds than by amending existing soil conditions. Over the existing soil spread a base of coarse rubble or stones; over this base, layer the planting medium of sand, gravel, compost and bagged garden soil mixed in equal parts; top the bed with a layer of pea gravel (which acts as a mulch). The planting layer should be at least 30 cm (12") thick, and thicker in areas of high rainfall and poor drainage. Edging helps to control erosion. The best fertilizer for desert plants is mineral-rich organic rock dust such as lava or granite sand worked into the soil twice a year; I also add a dry organic fertilizer.

It is not necessary to add irrigation to your dry bed. In regions where temperatures exceed 38°C (100°F), a weekly watering during hot spells may be needed, but in areas with regular rainfall your desert garden will not tolerate extra watering. Spring and fall cleanups are very important for providing plants with good air circulation. If possible, give plants much more space than is standard in a perennial border, both to enhance air circulation and to create the sparse look typical of drylands.

Plants for the desert garden

There is a wide variety of plant types to choose from, even if you live in cooler climate zones. The most important cautionary note for desert gardens where children will work or play is to avoid some of the really spiny or thorny plants. Some agaves are lethal, and yucca "Spanish Dagger" has earned its name. Although the plants recommended below work well across a range of climates, your local nursery should be able to help you determine the right plants for your area. The plants listed, with the exceptions noted, are all native to North America or Mexico.

Some of the *Agaves, Beschornerias, Dasylirions, Manfredas, Nolinas* and *Yuccas* are hardy to -18°C (0°F); some yuccas are hardy to -29°C (-20°F). One of my favorite dryland plants is red yucca (*Hesperaloe parviflora*). Its leaves are flexible and its flower stalks are striking and attractive to hummingbirds. It is easy to propagate from seed. *Yucca filamentosa* has broad, soft leaves accentuated by curling "hairs." I have agaves in my garden, situated against a wall where no one can fall against them; *Agave neomexicana* is very cold-hardy.

Of the succulents, sedum "Autumn Joy" (*Sedum telephium*) grows beautifully in my dryland garden, and is extremely cold-hardy. Moonstones (*Pachyphytum oviferum*), native to Mexico, and the African natives hens and chicks (*Sempervivums*) and velvet elephant ear (*Kalanchoe beharensis*), fit the dryland culture. They are fun and easy to grow in pots, but should be brought in during the winter to be protected from frost.

Certain cold-hardy cacti are worth searching out, especially the *Echinocereus spp.* and *Escobaria spp. Echinocereus triglochidiatus* has a large number of subspecies with different characteristics, while *E. viridiflorus* is native to prairies as far north as Wyoming, making it more tolerant of moist conditions. A small barrel cactus, *Escobaria missouriensis* is extremely cold-hardy and adaptable. I do not recommend most opuntias, which have spines that penetrate the skin.

While desert gardens tend to conjure images of cactus, herbaceous plants can flourish in the desert, too. In fact, many Mediterranean plants, such as rosemary, lavender and oregano, need dryland habitat. Native to South Africa, African daisy (*Gazania*) adapts well to dry beds. North American herbaceous natives such as salvias (*Salvia greggii*) and verbenas (*Verbena tenuisecta, V. bipinnatifida*) are good companions to the more sculptural desert plants. While these plants are not truly cold-hardy, they are good additions to the annual mix.

Grasses are perfectly suited to desert gardens. Lindheimer muhly (*Muhlenbergia lindheimerii*) is one of my favorites, with soft blue foliage and excellent drought tolerance. Blue fescue (*Festuca ovina*) is a low, clumping grass that provides nice contrast. Native to China and Japan, *Miscanthus spp.* are hardy across a wide range of climates and offer a variety of foliage types.

Teaching in the desert garden

The educational benefits of developing a desert garden are enormous. Environmental studies could highlight the use of native plants in drought conditions.

Janet Fox

The nice thing about desert gardens is that they can be large or small, depending on your location, budget and needs; even a series of pots can replicate the desert environment.

"Xeriscaping" is a relatively new concept, meaning the ecologically sensible choice of low-water-use plants and efficient water use wherever possible. A xeriscape garden is not necessarily a desert garden, but the principles can be taught by involving students in bed preparation, plant choice, and maintenance of the desert garden.

Drylands are also fascinating ecosystems, and students can have a close look at how rich a seemingly hostile environment can be (my own dry beds attract hummingbirds, butterflies, skinks, chameleons, tree frogs, toads and snakes). The ecology of drylands can be taught through a study of animal adaptations to deserts such as the creative ways animals have of escaping hot or dry conditions (nocturnal habit, burrowing, skin or body-type adaptations, methods of locomotion). Students can also observe the adaptations of plants to the low-water environment of your desert garden. For example, leaf shape and size, or the lack of true leaves on plants like the cacti and succulents, can be used to show how plants reduce transpiration or store water. Annuals can be used to demonstrate the opportunistic reproductive strategies of plants that spring to life only under the right conditions.

Your bed could provide a focus for the study of geography and geomorphology of drylands and deserts, as in the distribution of dryland environments in such diverse places as the Sahara and the Antarctic, or the typical desert landforms created by erosion. Art in the desert can include observing the sculptural forms of many desert plants. For a literature segment, a large number of children's books (some recommended below) are set in the desert environment. There are also fun projects for dryland beds. Your bed might incorporate a rock garden to highlight the teaching of geology. A sandy area that can be dug into for dinosaur "fossils" is fun for younger children. Rocks arranged in a decorative way — for example, spread along the ground in the shape of stone "snakes" — are eye-catching and may also serve to channel runoff or contain soil where necessary.

The desert garden is a captivating environment that will inspire you and your students. With the right plants you can recreate the desert look almost anywhere. And you can use desert gardens to teach principles of conservation and natural balance so essential to our students' futures. ❧

Dryland gardens are great places to learn about adaptations to low-water environments.

Janet Fox is a writer, an avid gardener, and the landscape chair of an educational garden at an elementary school in College Station, Texas.

Resources

Plant Materials:
Yucca Do Nursery, Route 3, Box 104, Hempstead, TX 77445, www.yuccado.com

High Country Gardens, 2902 Rufina St., Santa Fe, NM 87505-2929, www.highcountrygardens.com

Books on Dryland Plants and Environments:
Brookes, John. *Natural Landscapes.* New York: DK Publishing, 1998.

Christopher, Thomas. *Water-Wise Gardening.* New York: Simon & Schuster, 1994.

Ellefson, Connie, Tom Stephens and Doug Welsh. *Xeriscape Gardening.* New York: Macmillan, 1992.

Grantham, Keith and Paul Klaassen. *The Plantfinders Guide to Cacti and Other Succulents.* Portland, Oregon: Timber Press, 1999.

Phillips, Judith. *Plants for Natural Gardens: Southwestern Native and Adaptive Trees, Shrubs & Grasses.* Santa Fe: Museum of New Mexico Press, 1995.

Books for Teachers:
Braus, Judy, ed. *Ranger Ricks NatureScope: Discovering Deserts.* Washington, DC: National Wildlife Federation, 1989.

Books for Children:
Baylor, Byrd. *The Desert is Theirs.* New York: Charles Scribner's Sons, 1975.

Jernigan, Gisela. *One Green Mesquite Tree.* Tucson, Arizona: Harbinger House, 1988.

McLerran, Alice. *Roxaboxen.* New York: Lothrop, Lee & Shepard Books, 1991.

Pringle, Laurence. *The Gentle Desert.* New York: Macmillan, 1977.

Creating a Schoolyard Tree Nursery

by Cathy Dueck

W hile dreaming about the ideal schoolyard is inspiring and motivating, translating the dream into reality can be more difficult. If the object is to achieve instant and dramatic changes, there can be a large price tag attached, complete with a range of consultants and contractors. But there are simpler, more do-it-yourself approaches to bringing about positive changes in the schoolyard. One way is to start a school tree nursery. Although growing your own trees takes longer than buying them, seedlings grown in a clearly marked nursery area are much less prone to damage by trampling or mowing than those planted directly in their permanent sites; and when they are big enough to be transplanted, the trees will already be accustomed to the soil and weather in your schoolyard.

Growing your own trees is also a great way to encourage a lifelong friendship with a larger family of living things. When students are involved in collecting seeds and see the growth and development of seedlings over a period of time, they begin to understand that trees are dynamic, living things, and not just pieces of wood stuck in the ground. Through caring for young seedlings, they can learn to recognize different species, become familiar with what each needs to grow and thrive, and, as the trees grow bigger, participate in choosing suitable permanent planting locations. Growing trees is an adventure with no failures — just great opportunities to learn together and to play an important role in the processes of renewal and restoration.

Cathy Dueck

A small raised bed under dappled shade accommodates several hundred tiny trees.

Start small

You don't need much space to get started. It is surprising how many young trees can be grown in a small area. A growing bed 1 x 3 meters (3' x 10') can support roughly 20 to 30 young trees up to one meter high, or several hundred tiny trees in the first year or two of life. A space 3 x 3 meters (10' x 10') would provide enough room for two growing beds with walking paths all around.

Most important is to select a location that offers protection from sun and wind and access to water. An ideal location will have dappled shade: a touch of sun for plant growth, but not so much that the seedlings become dry and scorched. Commercial growers often put shade frames over young plants, simple frames covered with snow fencing. While young seedlings do not require a lot of care, they need regular watering. If you're lucky, Mother Nature will do the job for you. If not, make the task as simple as possible by choosing a location close to an outdoor faucet. If you are able to collect rainwater, that's even better.

Preparing a growing bed

Raised beds are recommended when working with children. Having the trees higher than the walking paths helps everyone remember where to walk and reduces soil compaction around the young trees. Growing beds should be no wider than one meter so that students can tend the plants from either side without stepping on the bed. Use boards or logs up to 20 cm (8") high to surround the bed, and add a light soil mix to fill it. You can dig up the soil that is already there (be sure to shake out and remove sod and weeds) and top it up with soil from the path area if necessary. Mix in about one-third compost or peat and a sprinkling of bone meal to promote healthy root growth. If your soil is heavy clay, some sand will help to loosen it up.

Seeds or transplants?

Some schools start by planting young trees from local growers or forest stations. These are not expensive, and sometimes are available free of charge to schools. You simply order the number and species you want and then transplant the tiny trees to the nursery when they arrive. Here, they get loving attention for one or two years and then are moved to a permanent planting site.

Another approach, which offers a better learning experience, is for students to grow trees from seed they have collected themselves. This is a great way to learn how and where trees grow, what is found in your area, and what kinds of plants usually grow together. Go for walks in nearby natural areas, taking along a good field guide or a local naturalist to help identify what's growing around you. Try to find a reference book that focuses on plants native to your bioregion, or call your local forest station to learn which trees are part of your heritage, and how to recognize them.

Cathy Dueck

Spring seeds

Each kind of tree has an optimum time of year for seed collection. There are several trees whose seeds mature in late spring or early summer, and most of these seeds will grow without much pampering. If you look closely, you will notice that many of these "early birds" produce their flowers before the leaves come out. The flowers tend to be small and unobtrusive, but you will see a flush of color on the tree for a week or two before the leaves unfold. Trees in this category include elm, silver maple, red maple, and poplars. Their seeds will be ripe in late spring, and you can often pick them right off the tree or collect them from the ground. Don't wait too long, though, or most of them will have blown away!

If you scatter the seeds over a prepared seed bed and keep them fairly moist, many will sprout without any coaxing. Young seedlings should not be allowed to dry out. You can reduce the workload by covering the soil surface with an organic material such as leaves, straw or wood chips. This will help to conserve water and keep down weed growth. Water only when the surface feels dry to the touch so you don't waterlog your seedlings. A watering can is a perfect way to deliver a gentle flow of water.

Be sure to label all trees and seeds. Waterproof markers on wooden stakes work well for this. Keep a paper map indoors of what you planted where, and when, in case the stakes are pulled up.

When students are involved in collecting seeds and see the growth and development of seedlings over a period of time, they begin to understand that trees are dynamic, living things, and not just pieces of wood stuck in the ground.

Fall seeds

Autumn is another important season for seed collection at school. The seeds of many trees ripen in the fall, and can be directly planted in the tree nursery at this time. Sugar maple, Manitoba maple, oaks, black walnut, and white ash can all be collected when the seeds are ripe, and planted directly outside in seed beds. You can also look for seeds inside the cones of evergreens such as pines, spruce and cedar, but they will blow away soon after the cones open up. Collect the cones just as they start to open and store them in a paper bag. This way, you can catch the seeds as they fall out.

Nuts, especially, must be protected from foraging squirrels by a wire cover (chicken wire or hardware cloth). If you're using raised growing beds, you can staple the wire directly onto the wooden frames. Many of these late ripening seeds need to be exposed to a cool winter period before they will grow. This is nature's way of ensuring that they wait until growing conditions are ideal. If all goes well, you will find lots of sprouts the following spring.

Long-term care

While young seedlings do not require much care, be sure not to forget about them. Arrange for families to share summer maintenance, and plan the occasional weeding bee. It's not good to let the weeds get taller than the trees! Spending a little time regularly ensures that the workload is pleasant and manageable.

If you find that your seeds sprout and grow up too close together, you can space them out when the weather is cool. Just dig up the seedlings, replant them a little farther apart, and water well. You may have to repeat this thinning process as the trees get bigger in the next year or two. The best time for transplanting is spring or fall when the trees are dormant.

By the time your trees are about one meter high, you'll probably want to move them to a permanent planting site or a bigger nursery area. Dig them up carefully in early spring or late fall, trim the roots a bit, and transplant them in the same way as for trees from commercial nurseries. Remember to replant the trees at the same depth they were growing in the nursery. A color change on the bark of the trunk will show you where ground level should be.

Pointers for success

Make sure that students are involved in the whole process. They will love going on excursions to collect seeds. When they've helped to plant and tend young trees in the nursery, they will also be more protective of the trees once they are planted out in the schoolyard.

Whenever possible, link curricular activities with the growth of the young trees. Which trees grow the fastest? Why? Do some get more shade than others? How does this affect their growth? Are any animals or insects munching on your trees? What clues do they leave behind? Are the same kinds of trees growing in your neighborhood? Where do they grow (wild, cultivated, wet, dry)? What other kinds of plants and animals can be found nearby?

As with any schoolyard project, involve as many people as possible. Make sure the caretakers know what you are doing and are supportive. Maybe they will even help to water now and then. Perhaps a parent in the community can help you identify trees or would love to help collect seeds. Members of local horticultural or field naturalist clubs can also be valuable resource people.

Growing trees from seed takes time but offers both economic and educational advantages that are missed when trees are simply purchased and delivered to the schoolyard. Starting a tree nursery is a wonderful foundation for schoolyard projects, a perfect way for students to learn basic skills before moving out into the larger schoolyard, and a fabulous opportunity to make positive links with the living world around us. ❧

Cathy Dueck is the Greenspace Coordinator for the Peterborough Green-Up project in Peterborough, Ontario.

Henry Kock

Seedlings grown in a clearly marked nursery area are much less prone to damage by trampling or mowing than those planted directly in their permanent sites; and when they are big enough to be transplanted, the trees will already be accustomed to the soil and weather in your schoolyard.

Rooftop Gardens

Rooftops are a city's greatest untapped resource — acres and acres of empty space just waiting to be used! Imagine driving along an urban freeway and looking out over a sea of green instead of the sea of tar, asphalt, and gravel that we now have. Imagine looking out of a downtown office window and seeing meadows of indigenous wildflowers instead of air-handling units and roof vents. Imagine growing vegetables on top of that garage that takes up most of your backyard. This vision is not so far-fetched or so far-off as it may seem. In Europe, where sprawl is no longer possible and higher population densities have made the environmental crisis more immediate, roof greening has been adopted as much out of necessity as out of a wish to beautify the urban landscape. In fact, roof greening is now legislated for new industrial buildings in many northern European cities, and strongly recommended for others.

by Monica Kuhn

Green Roofs for Healthy Cities Coalition, www.peck.ca/grhcc/main.htm

So how about a green roof on top of your school — a school garden that is safe from vandalism and receives full exposure to sunlight; an outdoor classroom where children can learn first-hand about weather, plants, and the benefits of integrating the natural with the human-made. Grow vegetables and you can supply food for the cafeteria; grow flowers and you can attract butterflies. Sloped or flat, large or small, rooftops offer limitless possibilities for urban greening, environmental education, community building, and the creation of safe outdoor spaces.

Cover any roof with plants and you have immediately achieved several things. Environmentally, by increasing the biomass in the city, you have increased oxygen levels and decreased carbon dioxide. Plants act as natural filters, so you have also cut down on dust and airborne particulates. Since plants absorb rather than reflect heat, you have had a hand in altering the local climate; and because plant roots hold and absorb water, your roof retains storm water, thereby decreasing the load on the city's already overflowing storm sewage system.

The economic benefits are also substantial. Layers of soil and foliage have wonderful insulating qualities, keeping the building warmer in the winter and cooler in the summer, thereby reducing the energy bill. Since extreme temperature swings are moderated, the degree of expansion and contraction of the roof decreases; and because the roofing is covered, the membrane is protected from harmful ultraviolet rays and everyday wear and tear, which increases its life span and reduces replacement and repair costs.

Monica Kuhn

Rooftop gardens enjoy full sun and are safe from vandalism.

On an educational and social level, an accessible rooftop green space can be used as a laboratory for experimentation, an outdoor place for play and performance, a school garden, or just a quiet area to read and write. Green roofs can also promote community activities. A common problem with school gardening is that the growing season is just getting started when the school year finishes and no one is there to take care of the garden through the summer. This can be turned into an opportunity to forge links with local community groups, seniors' programs, children's daycares or summer day camps who would love to have a place to garden. Spring planting and fall harvesting can become combined school and community events which extend the teaching and learning far beyond the classroom. Gaining support, funding, and donations of labor and materials is made easier if the garden is open to a larger community.

Green roofs can be divided into two distinct types: the vegetation-covered or "inaccessible" roof, and the roof garden or "accessible" roof. Inaccessible green roofs are those on which vegetation acts just like another layer of roofing material. They are meant to be looked at, not walked upon, can be installed on flat as well as sloped roofs, require little maintenance, and, depending on climate and rainfall, can support a variety of hardy grasses, wildflowers, mosses, and sedums in a soil layer as thin as 8 cm (3"). Accessible green roofs, on the other hand, are essentially outdoor rooms, and as such fall under the restrictions of building codes with respect to public safety features such as exits, guardrails, and lighting. They are usually installed on flat roofs, for obvious reasons, with the vegetation either as a "carpet" or in containers and raised beds, separated by areas of decking. The weight and carrying capacity of the roof structure often play a greater role in the design of an accessible green roof due to the added load of people, containers, decking, trees, and deeper soil; installation and maintenance costs increase accordingly.

If you are interested in growing a green roof on your school, there are several technical issues that you should be aware of.

Safety

The first consideration is safety.

↝ How will you and the students get to the roof: interior stairs, exterior stairs, ladder, elevator, ramp? Can everyone get down quickly and safely if they have to?

↝ Does your access already exist or will you have to install it? Will it meet the requirements of the building code?

↝ How will you get materials, plants, and water up to the roof: stairwell, elevator, exterior hoist, ladder, window?

↝ Can you install a hosebib? Can you collect rainwater?

↝ Who will be using the roof: teachers, students, staff, parents, community members, the handicapped? How many people will be on the roof at one time?

↝ Is there a railing and is it the correct height?

↝ Are you insured?

Bylaws and building codes have regulations governing structure, use, and safety. A call to the design department at your school board will help to get things started.

Loading

The second consideration is loading. The weight of soil, decking, people, and planters — and where they are placed — will all depend on the structural capacity of the roof and the rest of the building. Again, be sure to consult with your local board. They will probably need to have a structural engineer confirm the additional weight that the roof can accommodate. One cubic foot of wet "earth" weighs approximately 45 kilograms (100 pounds), so you can imagine the additional stresses that a garden can create. However, remember that earth is not soil: you will probably be adding compost, mulch, and other fillers which will decrease the weight. Nor do all of your planting beds have to be 30 cm (12") deep; nor will you be covering the whole roof surface. Heavy planters can be placed strategically over bearing walls or columns; grasses do not need more than 8 cm (3") of growing medium; some plants will grow in gravel.... You have a lot of options.

Roofing

The third consideration is roofing.

↝ What kind of roofing system do you have? Each has distinct characteristics: some are not made to be continuously wet, others are; some are made with organic

An accessible rooftop green space can be used as a laboratory for experimentation, an outdoor place for play and performance, a school garden, or just a quiet area to read and write.

materials and are thus very attractive to plant roots; some may react chemically with materials in your garden; and some need to be protected from ultraviolet rays.

↝ What condition is your roof membrane in? If you have to replace or repair it within five years, can you do so without disrupting your established garden? Maybe your garden should be compartmentalized for easy access and repair.

↝ Can you walk on the roofing, or should it be protected with wood decking, pavers, rigid insulation, gravel, or grass?

↝ Will plant roots penetrate the membrane or should you plant in elevated planters?

↝ How and where does the roof drain? Filter cloth to keep the soil from eroding with the water is a must.

Again, talk to the board, landscapers, designers, or a roofing contractor. Although it may seem complex, there are as many solutions as there are restrictions or potential problems.

Roof micro-climate

Fourth, consider the micro-climate of the roof itself. Gardening up on a roof is quite different from gardening at ground level. It is very sunny, sometimes windy, and the temperatures are often extreme. This will have a direct effect on what will grow well, how often you have to water, and whether your plants can survive through the winter. Greenhouses and cold frames are life savers. You can also temper the effects of heat, cold, and dryness by using plastic containers that retain moisture instead of terra cotta; by insulating your planters; by using mulch; by mixing moisture-retaining additives into your soil; by layering or interplanting your plants; or by sticking to plants that thrive in these conditions. You can build trellises and shade structures; you can collect rainwater. This is likely to be an ongoing experiment!

Green rooftop on the Steiner Kindergarten in Wales.

Rooftop plants

Last, but not least, consider the plants. What you plant and what will prosper depend on how much time you are willing to dedicate to the garden. If you are looking for a maintenance-free installation, the climate and lack of water will often limit plant selection to hardier or indigenous varieties. Root size and depth are also important. Will the plant be able to stabilize and flourish in 10 cm (4") or does it need 60 cm (24") of soil? Are the conditions in which the plants were grown comparable to the conditions you will be subjecting them to? Typically, inaccessible roofs use a mixture of grasses, mosses, sedums, sempervivums, festucas, irises — plants that are native to drylands, tundra, and alpine slopes. On an accessible roof, with few exceptions, the choices are limitless. In Europe there are nurseries that specialize in providing plants specifically for green roof installations. Here we are still experimenting. Consult a landscape architect or horticulturist for advice.

Each roof is as different as the gardener who uses it or the building on which it is built. There are already many schools throughout the world that have been capped in green, with remarkable benefits to the students as well as to the surrounding communities. The next time you think about greening your city, look up towards the rooftops. You will be surprised at the hints of green and growing things that you can see. ❦

Monica Kuhn is a registered architect in Toronto, Ontario, who specializes in rooftop gardens and permaculture design. She is a founding member of the Rooftop Gardens Resource Group (http://www.interlog.com/~rooftop/), a volunteer organization helping to design and implement green rooftops in Toronto.

Bob Johnson

Attracting wildlife

🍃 **Whatever Happened to the "Wild" in Kids' Lives?** by Edward Cheskey

🍃 **The Foundation of Habitat: Native Plants** by David Mizejewski

🍃 **Amphibian Oasis** by Heather Gosselin and Bob Johnson

🍃 **Avian Attraction** by Ken Quanz and Edward Cheskey

🍃 **Projects for the Birds** by Steven Uriarte

🍃 **Butterfly Gardens** by Kim Denman

Whatever Happened to the "Wild" in Kids' Lives?

by Edward Cheskey

The movement to naturalize schoolyards has many motives, one of which is a desire to increase opportunities for students to observe wildlife. The important role that schoolyard wildlife habitats can play in fostering a relationship between children and nature is underscored when we consider the dominance of the social forces that have eroded this relationship in recent decades.

One such force is the concentration of people into cities. During the 20th century in North America the proportion of the total population living in urban centers shifted from about 30 percent to about 80 percent. The very concept of the city is based on separating people from the land, and the ecology of cities reinforces this separation. As Gary Nabhan puts it, "[cities] are not even designed to be habitable for other species, so that the weeds or English sparrows or Norway rats we find there survive despite our efforts to eradicate them." Cities are inhospitable places for wildlife due to their:

Ray Cromie

- *Low primary productivity.* Roads, buildings, and parking lots cover much of the land surface in cities.

- *Predominance of lawns.* Lawns of one or two types of grass, kept short by mowing, support few forms of life and offer little shelter.

- *Impaired hydrology.* Cities are hydrological disasters. Major engineering efforts to channel water away from buildings also keep water from going into the ground, thus lowering water tables while increasing the flow of surface water. Surface water is often contaminated with toxins from automobiles, equipment and factories. Wetlands are drained and littoral habitats are filled to accommodate industrial or residential expansion. Standing water is considered a liability.

- *Constant disturbance.* Most places in cities have high levels of human activity to which most species are poorly adapted.

- *High levels of pollution.* Air, water, and soil pollution reduce productivity and diversity.

Creating habitats to support wildlife in cities depends on addressing these ecological problems. For example, increasing the productivity and diversity of vegetation increases the number of available niches. Birds and other highly mobile organisms such as butterflies respond quickly to increases in plant diversity.

A second force which alienates children from nature is the change in information and communication technologies. Television, and now computers, take up increasing amounts of children's time. Recent studies indicate that by the time they finish high school children have spent more time watching television than attending school. As our culture has become myopically obsessed with these technologies, we have lost perspective of nature. Observing wildlife will probably not, for most children, become an alternative to television. But given frequent opportunities to watch, listen, and observe the behavior of other creatures, children will find that every species is a fascinating story in itself.

A third force is the instability caused by the globalization of our economy. Centralized corporate decisions to shift production and move capital ultimately mean that many people have little choice any more in where they live. Frequent career changes and the transience of families leave a large sector of the population unable to set down roots in any one place. Children lose out in these situations because they do not have time to develop long-term relationships. We all hear how adaptable children are, but at what cost? An interest in nature is one of the best gifts that one can give to a child because wherever that child goes, he or she will find interest, awe, and comfort in the nature of the new place. The prospect of discovering what other creatures are living around you, be they birds, snakes, mammals, or insects, can be an unending thread of excitement and enjoyment throughout life.

The final force is the very nature of the market economy in which everything from food to love is treated as a commodity. Everything, it seems, has a price. In this cultural milieu, nature, too, becomes something to be traded and sold. The trend toward valuing living things only as commodities is the ultimate alienation of humans from the rest of nature. To counter this market view of the world, we need to develop and promote awareness of the emotional and spiritual value of nature.

These major cultural tendencies leave few opportunities for children to observe and interact with wildlife. As educators we should consider strategically how we can help children build a strong environmental ethic when so many factors are undermining our efforts. This ethic has to find its way past children's heads and into their hearts, and it can do so only when nature is experienced as part of the life of each child. Creating opportunities for regular contact with wildlife through schoolyard habitat restoration is a main ingredient in this strategy. A study of wildlife is a study of life itself; it can be used to infuse environmental ethics into almost every subject curriculum. ❧

Edward Cheskey is a bird conservation planner with the Federation of Ontario Naturalists in Guelph, Ontario.

An interest in nature is one of the best gifts that one can give to a child because wherever that child goes, he or she will find interest, awe, and comfort in the nature of the new place.

The Foundation of Habitat: Native Plants

by David Mizejewski

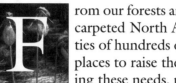

From our forests and prairies to our deserts and wetlands, plants have carpeted North America for millions of years. As mixed communities of hundreds of species, plants provide wildlife with food, cover, places to raise their young, and in some cases even water. In fulfilling these needs, plants form the foundation of habitat for wildlife.

Over geologic time, the distribution of plants and the wildlife that depends on them has changed repeatedly. Species have evolved, some flourishing and some becoming extinct over the course of millions of years. Over these immense time periods, the life cycles of plants and animals in a given region have evolved to complement each other. Migratory animals travel between ranges at the same time their plant food sources are producing the most food; animals have developed hibernation behavior that coincides with plant dormancy; and plants offer blooms that take advantage of the life cycles and physical shapes of their wildlife pollinators.

As the human population has increased and expanded, we have removed the plant communities in the regions we have inhabited and replaced them with plant species from other parts of the world. Most of this has happened in the last few centuries. In other words, in a few hundred years we have begun to unravel the intricate tapestry of the plant-animal relationship that took millions of years to develop. Many species of wildlife will not be able to adapt to these unnaturally rapid changes and may be threatened with extinction. Habitat loss is the number one threat to wildlife in North America today.

Native plants are simply the plants that evolved over time to the weather patterns, soil types, temperature extremes and wildlife of a given geographic region. A non-native or exotic plant is one that has been introduced, through human activity, to an area that it otherwise would not be able to reach. Human culture depends on non-native plants. Our food crops come from all parts of the world. We make many important products, from rubber to medicines to clothing, from cultivated species that are planted outside their natural ranges. However, our dependence on non-native plants has begun to threaten wildlife as our gardens and landscapes — along with our pesticides, chemical fertilizers, and domestic animals — encroach ever further into formerly wild places.

There are hundreds of species of non-native plants, mostly from Europe, Asia, Africa and Australia, that now cover North American landscapes and which cannot adequately sustain wildlife. (There are also North American species that are being planted well out of their original range.) In addition, non-native plants have a strong potential to become invasive. Some native plants are aggressive and will readily spread, but this behavior is within the balance of the local ecology and the natural succession of plant communities. Invasive plants, on the other hand, are non-native

Ted Walke

plants that out-compete native plants and spread rampantly. Often a handful of these introduced invasive species will replace entire native plant communities composed of hundreds of species. The end result is destruction of the habitat of hundreds of wildlife species that depended on those native plants.

A wildlife habitat garden provides an excellent opportunity to educate students on a wide range of topics. The most obvious is the opportunity to learn about the local ecology through first-hand observation of plant-animal interactions and life cycles. Lessons can focus on individual species to demonstrate processes such as metamorphosis, symbiosis, camouflage, reproduction and population dynamics. One of the most important educational elements that a wildlife friendly landscape with a native plant foundation can provide is a strong conservation message. By identifying the plants and animals in their own unique part of the world, students will learn the importance of preserving and restoring natural areas and will be imparted with a sense of place. This is increasingly important in our fast-paced, technology-driven culture.

Wildlife habitat areas can also be used in a multidisciplinary fashion. Students can learn writing skills by keeping a nature journal, calculation and graphing skills by monitoring plant growth, cultural history by focusing on the plants and animals that were historically important, art and design through plant choice and arrangement, and even carpentry and tool use through the installation process. Habitat projects can also serve as a springboard for studying environmental issues such as organic gardening, integrated pest management, water and air pollution, human population growth and suburban sprawl.

The horticultural industry is just beginning to recognize the value of working with native plants. This means that finding native plants for your habitat project may not always be as easy as a trip to the local garden center. Many nurseries that do have native plants offer only specially selected or cloned cultivars and varieties that have been selected for their showy blooms or disease resistance, but not their value to wildlife. Whenever possible, choose the pure species for your habitat. Also, never collect from the wild, unless it is part of an authorized plant rescue (usually from a development site). Many species have been pushed to the brink of extinction as a result of wild collection. ❧

David Mizejewski is the manager of the Backyard Wildlife Habitat Program of the National Wildlife Federation in Vienna, Virginia.

For information on how to start a wildlife habitat project and sources for plants that are native to your region, contact National Wildlife Federation at (703) 790-4100 or visit www.nwf.org/habitats.

Some native plants are aggressive and will readily spread, but this behavior is within the balance of the local ecology and the natural succession of plant communities. Invasive plants, on the other hand, are non-native plants that out-compete native plants and spread rampantly.

Designing and building a schoolyard pond

Amphibian Oasis

by Heather Gosselin and Bob Johnson

Since the issue of declining amphibian populations was first raised at the First World Congress of Herpetology in 1989, the decline or disappearance of amphibian species has been documented around the world. Scientists suggest that the sensitive skin of larval and adult amphibians makes them vulnerable to changes in air and water, including contamination by herbicides and pesticides, acid rain, and increases in ultraviolet light. Amphibians can thus be considered "barometers" of the environment and their disappearance a warning of environmental change.

Building a schoolyard pond is one of the most rewarding ways of helping to boost local populations of amphibians and one of the best methods of increasing the natural value and visual appeal of school grounds. If designed properly, a pond will allow you to observe the life cycles of plants, invertebrates, and amphibians. In what follows, we outline many of the important considerations in designing and building a pond, with particular emphasis on meeting the needs of amphibians.

Michelle Barraclough

Choosing a site

Ideally, you should locate your pond where it can receive meltwater. Look for low ground that naturally collects water and where pools form in the spring. Water can be directed to this area or retained behind a low dam or berm. A good first step would be to talk to a local contractor or naturalist who can advise you on your local conditions.

Choose a sunny spot away from trees and tree roots, compost piles, and lawns treated with fertilizers. Excess nutrient release from organic matter or fertilizer may cause the water to lose clarity and become foul. Ammonia, released by many fertilizers during wet periods, has been found to affect tadpoles. Also consider whether amphibians will be able to enter and exit your pond without risking death. There are many incidences of toads, unable to climb concrete road curbs, suffering a high death rate due to vehicles or, in one case, being swept up into a road sweeper each morning of the week. Locating the pond away from roads and, ideally, adjacent to a ravine or wooded area will make your pond a safer and more inviting habitat for amphibians.

The closer the pond is to existing wetlands with established amphibian populations, the more likely that some will take up residence and actually breed in the new pond. Nearby rivers, creeks, and irrigation ditches, especially those with ponds and vegetation along the banks and occasional adjacent ponds, are ideal breeding grounds and dispersal routes for frogs and toads.

Holding in the water

If your soil particle size is small (sandy, silty soils) with a clay content of at least 10 percent, then soil compaction is the easiest way of sealing the bottom of your pond. If the soil in your area does not contain clay, you will need an impervious layer to hold the pond water. Pre-molded fiberglass, concrete, clay or flexible pool liners can be used for this purpose.

Clay liners: You can create a clay liner by importing soils with a clay content of more than 20 percent for compaction, or by purchasing bentonite clay. Although

Attracting Wildlife

clay-lined ponds are the most natural looking, clay is not the best choice of impermeable pond barriers. It is very heavy and can leak if not installed correctly.

Concrete ponds: Concrete ponds are expensive, requiring the installation of footings, reinforcements, and several inches of solid concrete that is best handled by professionals. And although concrete ponds should have a long lifespan, it is not uncommon to find cracking within a few years.

Fiberglass ponds: Several small fiberglass pools can be placed side by side around a central land area that is heavily planted to create one wetland. However, a fiberglass pond is expensive and requires brick sand to be packed underneath to ensure good drainage. This prevents water from becoming trapped below the fiberglass, which causes it to cork or come up out of the ground. Many of the so-called "frog ponds" sold by nurseries in pre-packaged boxes are solid fiberglass. These are deep, with very steep sides, and are death traps to amphibians that may fall in and cannot climb out of the water. Remember to place rocks or logs in deep or steep-sided pools so that toadlets and froglets can climb out.

Flexible pond liners: Flexible liners are the best choice for schoolyard ponds because they are relatively inexpensive and can be installed by do-it-yourselfers. There are four main types of flexible pond liners: 40 to 80 mil PVC sheeting, rubberized pool liners, 45 mil High Density Polyethylene (HDPE) liners, and 45 mil Ethylene Propylene Diene Monomer (EPDM) liners. Most of these are manufactured in black and natural tones of brown and green, creating a more natural look for your pond.

While each type of liner has advantages, we recommend the 45 mil EPDM liner. PVC liners may crack during the winter and are difficult to patch; rubberized liners are expensive and contain toxic substances that may leach into the water; and HDPE liners are difficult to work with in cold climates. The 45 mil EPDM liners are flexible, UV-stable, resistant to air pollution, non-toxic to pond life, very inexpensive, and have a lifespan of 20 years. They are also proven to be the best liner for a cold climate. Whatever liner you choose, check that a patching kit is available!

It is best to decide the type of liner you want and to see what sizes it comes in before deciding on the shape and size of your pond. A number of bulk liner rolls come in increments of 1.5 meters (5'), starting at the 3-meter (10') width. To determine what size of liner you will need, measure the length and width of the rectangle that your pool fits in. Add twice the maximum depth of your pond and then add one meter to each of these measurements and you have the size of the liner you need. In other words:

1 + (2 x maximum depth) + length = length in meters (x 3.3 = length in feet)
1 + (2 x maximum depth) + width = width in meters (x 3.3 = width in feet)

Directing overflow

To prevent flooding, an overflow area should be built beyond the edge of your pond. This overflow consists of a hole dug down to a free-draining layer which is broken up, backfilled with clean stones or bricks and covered with a filter and topsoil. The filter should be a piece of old carpet, fiber matting or a layer of turf laid upside-down. Vegetation suitable for a wet meadow can be planted in the overflow area. If your pond is built on uneven ground, make sure the overflow is on the lower end.

Designing your pond

Amphibian ponds should be no smaller than 4 meters long and 2 meters (13' x 6.5') wide and at least 0.5 meters (18") deep. Ideally, the pond should be 6 meters long and 4 meters wide (20' x 13') . While this size may be intimidating, once set in

Building a schoolyard pond is one of the most rewarding ways of helping to boost local populations of amphibians and one of the best methods of increasing the natural value and visual appeal of school grounds.

the ground and planted around the edges to create terrestrial habitat, your pond will not appear to be so large. Amphibians are attracted to a pond by the size of its reflective surface. If the pond surface is too small, amphibians won't even notice it! Smaller ponds also suffer from temperature fluctuations and take longer to become settled and balanced. There must be enough bacteria and algae on rocks and on the bottom to feed tadpoles, and sufficient aquatic insect production to feed the adult frogs or toads. You will also want to have a pond big enough and deep enough to prevent predators such as crows, garter snakes, and raccoons from gaining access to the center of the pond. Most amphibians will rest or bask along the edges of a pond but retreat to deeper water when frightened.

The depth of the pond will also depend on whether or not the amphibian species in your area hibernate under water. If so, they will not survive in your pond if it completely freezes. To avoid this problem, dig at least one section below the frost line, or plan to install a pond aerator to prevent thick ice from forming. Amphibian species which hibernate under water include the bullfrog, pickerel frog, mink frog, green frog, northern leopard frog, mudpuppy, and the redspotted newt.

Although ponds can be created in many unusual shapes, it is best to stay away from too many curves and corners. It is difficult to fold most flexible liners into unusual shapes, and water ends up stagnating in the convolutes. Crescents or ovals are recommended.

Two wetlands in one: To create a bog as well as a pond, students at W.A. Porter Collegiate Institute in Scarborough, Ontario, divided their pond and filled one side with peat. Here, bog species such as horsetail and marsh marigold are set into the peat, while on the pond side are lilies and a variety of oxygenating plants.

Alternating shoreline depths allows you to create different habitats such as a wet meadow, a rock garden, and a cattail area. A shallow 10 to 18 cm (4"-7") deep shoreline or shelf provides growing areas for emergent plants and spawning areas for egg laying. In winter the shallow bank will allow ice to expand out of the pond, preventing damage to the liner.

Finally, be sure to check any local regulations related to the size and depth of schoolyard ponds. In some cases, school board regulations on depth are more stringent than local bylaws. To enhance safety for small children, you may want to restrict access with a natural-looking fence (such as cedar rail) and gate. Alternatively, you can submerge large rocks just below the water line to restrict access to deeper water. The rocks also provide a refuge for frogs and their tadpoles and may make it easier for wildlife to enter and exit the pond. Whether or not access is restricted, you can use the pond to teach water safety. An awareness of the potential danger and how to act responsibly around water will benefit both children and the wildlife that depend upon water for survival.

Digging your pond

Before you start digging your pond, it's a good idea to outline the proposed area with a piece of rope or flexible hose. You must also take into consideration the locations of any overhead or underground lines, and local bylaws requiring fencing or permits.

Natural debris removed during the digging may be useful for creating wildlife habitat around your pond. When stripping off the turf, save large pieces to be put around the edge of the pond. Digging should be done in layers so that the topsoil can be kept in a separate pile and used later.

Level the sides of the pond excavation by using pegs, a straight board, and a spirit level to make sure the water will rise to the same level on all sides. Reshape the surroundings to blend in before digging the depth of the pond. The pond must be excavated to a depth allowing for a waterproof barrier with its protective matting (if required) and for a layer of sand and gravel at least 8 cm (3") deep to cover the whole pond bed.

Attracting Wildlife

Installing a flexible pond liner

When you build your pond, pick a sunny day with no rain in the forecast for a couple of days. Sun makes digging more fun, but also warms up the pond liner, making it a little more malleable. Do not leave your liner out on the lawn in the sun, because the heat generated under it can kill large areas of grass.

Before installing the liner, check it for manufacturing defects such as holes and weak points. Remove all sharp objects from the excavation and make sure the soil is packed down hard and level. Line the hole with 5 cm (2") of sand and stretch the liner over it. It is advisable to have four people to help position the liner. Each can take a corner and make sure it is equally distributed over the pond. Place it over the hole and hold the sides firmly with a line of bricks or paving stones (see diagram). Place a garden hose in the middle of the pond and fill it with water. The weight of the water will settle the liner to the shape of the pool. While the pool is filling with water, someone should be in it with their shoes and socks off helping the liner fold in the corners. They should also ensure that the liner is not being pulled down unevenly as this can create a leak when the pond is filled up to level. Once filled, water pressure will prevent the liner from snapping back. This is the time to make final adjustments, such as levelling the liner edge, or to direct overflow to an intended area. Tuck the edge of the liner under 15 cm (6") of soil or keep it hidden underneath stones.

Once the pond liner is put in, the bottom should be covered with 2-10 cm (1"-4") of washed sand topped with a layer of gravel. Plant with aquatic vegetation. Until there is sufficient sediment to grow rooted plants, potted plants can be placed underwater along the edge or you can add a loam substrate. Submerged, aquatic plants are important egg laying sites and provide cover for frogs and tadpoles. Include an island of rocks or a weathered stump set in about one meter from the edge as resting areas for frogs, safe from predators such as raccoons. Plant native plants around the pond edge to provide cover for adults and emerging toadlets.

Water source

If you are filling your new pond with tap water, let it stand a week before transferring plants and animals to allow the chlorine to dissipate. Chlorine, commonly found in municipal water supplies, can kill tadpoles and other amphibious larvae. Placing your hose at an angle to create a spray while filling your pond increases the rate at which chlorine evaporates out of the water. There is no need to purchase de-chlorinating chemicals. Do check, however, to find out if your municipality has changed from using chlorine to chloramine, a chemical that does not dissipate out of water. If so, use a chloramine neutralizer to avoid losing all the wildlife in your pond.

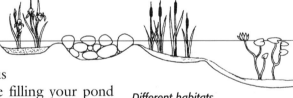

Different habitats are created by varying the depth and using sand, loam or rock substrates.

If you have a water meter, take a reading before and after you fill the pond to determine exactly how much water it holds. To top up your pond, you can use tap water if you are not adding any more than 10 percent of the total water volume, but it is preferable to use collected rainwater or water that has been standing over a week. Use water as close to the temperature of your pond as possible because sudden temperature changes of more than 5° C (10° F) will kill aquatic wildlife. If your pond is located near a building, redirect downspout water to replenish the pond each time it rains. If you have an underground water supply, you can attach a float valve which automatically tops up your pond as it loses water to evaporation.

If you are considering diverting water from natural streams or using waterways as sources of water, you should consult local authorities. There may be regulations in place to protect local fish stocks and water supplies.

Maintaining your pond

Once a pond becomes a balanced unit, annual care and maintenance should be minimal. Remove organic matter such as fallen leaves, needles, and dead stalks in the spring and fall to prolong the period between major cleanings.

All ponds will have algae and this is a natural component of all wetlands. Algae that is attached to rocks and the sides of your pond provide most of the pond's oxygen and are the most important food source for tadpoles. However, green water is caused by microscopic algae living in the water column. You cannot create a "balanced" wetland in a few days. Your pond will require time to reach its own internal balance and for nutrients which may increase algae growth to be used up by all the plants. Do not use algicides as they are only a short-term cure and can harm aquatic organisms. Oxygenating plants submerged in your pond will help to keep the nutrient cycle balanced by competing with algae for nitrogen and other nutrients in the water. Emergent or floating-leafed plants also take up nutrients and reduce light penetration into the pond and to the algae. The extra cover provided by the floating-leafed plants may also reduce evaporation and the temperature of your pond.

Bob Johnson

After one or two frogs or toads breed in the new pond, their offspring will return year after year to breed in the habitat that you have created.

Algal blooms often occur in the spring due to nutrient runoff and the lack of shading from plants. You can try to prevent nutrients from entering the water. Otherwise, you will have to wait until plant growth shades the pond, retarding algal growth, or until nutrients are used up by the rooted plants. During this time you can remove the excess algae by lifting it out with a rake or by placing a stick in the middle of the algae mass and twirling it onto the stick. Before placing the excess algae into your compost pile, make sure there are no amphibian eggs or tadpoles caught in it! To prevent this from occurring, the algae can be flushed in a bucket of water first.

All ponds need time to develop into good amphibian habitat. New ponds cannot replace the complex ecosystems of established wetlands. The quality of habitat is improved when plants and algae are well established, when sediments that cloud the water have settled to the bottom and stay there even after heavy rain, and when a nice layer of detritus (decomposed plant and animal matter) settles on the bottom of the pond. This is a source of nutrients for plants, tadpoles, and other aquatic organisms.

Be prepared for the possibility that no matter how good your new pond is, there may be no nearby amphibian populations to colonize it. *Do not deplete tadpoles from nearby sources to stock new ponds.* With prior approval from local conservation authorities, naturalists, or wildlife experts, you may move some (about 100 per year) toad or green frog tadpoles from a pond that is within three kilometers (two miles) of your location. Ensure that your pond is suitable for that species and that you will not be depleting tadpoles from a source population that is itself in trouble.

Even if your new pond is close to existing wetlands, amphibians are creatures of habit and will not at first want to move from their old breeding pond to a new one. However, after one or two frogs or toads breed in the new pond, their offspring will return year after year to breed in the habitat that you have created. In a new pond, toads are often the first species of amphibian to appear. They adapt very well to living around homes and gardens, and are a good species to attract to your new schoolyard pond. And while you are waiting for the first toads to arrive, take delight in the first dragonfly that magically arrives at your new wetland. ❧

Heather Gosselin is past coordinator of the Adopt-a-Pond Programme and Bob Johnson is the Curator of Amphibians and Reptiles at the Toronto Zoo in Toronto, Ontario.

Avian Attraction

by Ken Quanz and
Edward Cheskey

Glory be to God for dappled things —
For skies of couple-color as a brindled cow;
For rose-moles all in stipple upon trout that swim;
Fresh-firecoal chestnut-falls; finches' wings. . .
— Gerard Manley Hopkins, "Pied Beauty"

The animation, ubiquity, and familiarity of birds make them an ideal subject for focusing students' attention on nature. In urban areas, highly adapted and tolerant wildlife can be found virtually anywhere, and birds are by far the most conspicuous of these. The house sparrow, European starling and rock dove (pigeon) are year-round resident implants from Europe that have evolved closely with humans over millennia. Other species indigenous to North America have also adapted to human settlement: the American robin, American crow, blue jay and black-capped chickadee come to mind as ones that do well in the typical suburb or city park. But many others require special habitat and landscape features that are sadly lacking in urban environments. As a result, few schoolyards could attract and sustain many species beyond ring-billed gulls, starlings and the occasional robin. This does not have to be the case because attracting birds to the schoolyard is not difficult. As the architects say, build it and they will come.

Habitat is the single greatest factor in attracting a variety of species of birds. How many times have you driven through a new, barren subdivision and seen bird feeders full of seed, but no birds? If we look at the basic habitat needs of all living things — food, water, shelter, and space — it quickly becomes obvious that attracting birds requires more than supplying food. Many species need forests, meadows, ponds, and wetlands to address water and territory requirements; and most birds will rarely venture, even for food, into areas that do not offer sheltering vegetation and distance from human disturbance. Many school grounds resemble new subdivisions: there are few trees, fewer shrubs, and no herbaceous plants other than short-cropped grass. A schoolyard naturalization project is an excellent opportunity for creating a diverse habitat that will benefit not only the human inhabitants, but the feathered ones as well. The following outlines some important considerations in creating bird habitat at your school.

Locating your feeders

Most birds require an element of safety while they are at a feeder: there must be a safe place close by to escape to if a predator is spotted. Trees or shrubs should be thick enough to provide a refuge from a passing hawk, and tall enough to provide an escape from the neighborhood cats (which are a major problem in human habitats). Some birds such as mourning doves will feed only on the ground or on a platform, and will stay away if there is a good hiding spot for a cat nearby. Even if *you* believe there to be no cats or hawks, the birds must still be assured and protected. Use thick brambles or low fencing to limit the opportunity for cats to hide beneath shrubs and decks.

Since each species has different shelter needs, it is wise to provide a variety of vegetation near feeders. Conifers with dense foliage, such as cedars, are very important to many species because they offer both a refuge from predators and adequate cover for roosting during the night. Nest boxes, too, serve as night shelters which may be used by cavity nesters even during non-breeding seasons. If building nest boxes, limit the size of the opening to 3.8 cm (1.5") to discourage house sparrows and starlings, and leave off the classic perch below the entrance, or you will be inadvertently advertising for house sparrows.

In addition to providing shelter from predators, consider the features and uses of areas adjacent to the feeding site. Even when food and shelter are adequate, isolation and disturbance can render apparently good habitat unsuitable. Many school neighborhoods have natural features that enhance bird habitat such as lines of trees, ravines or streams, woodlands, meadows, or waterfronts. Planting trees or hedge rows that link your site to these areas will create a corridor that will facilitate the movement of birds to the school grounds. While proximity to natural sites will help to attract birds, boisterous human disturbance will tend to have the opposite effect. Ball and running games are bound to conflict with the birds, but most schoolyards are large enough that it is possible to situate bird habitats away from such activities. This is not to say that a feeding area cannot be used for quieter pursuits: an arrangement of benches where students can sit and talk, eat lunch, or play table games such as chess or checkers would qualify as a good human use of the feeder area.

Ideally, feeders should be near a classroom or library window where the birds will not be disturbed but can be watched from inside. If your feeder is near a window, attach hawk silhouettes to the window or keep the drapes partially closed to let the birds know there is glass there. In cases where the reflectivity of glass poses a major threat, consider hanging nylon mesh in front of the window.

Birds of prey are regularly attracted to a successful feeder, and an attack by a hawk, kestrel, or merlin can be a dramatic event to witness. An occasional consequence of an attack, however, is that a fleeing bird will inadvertently crash into a windowpane in attempting to evade the attacker. This is often fatal, especially in winter. Even if the unfortunate bird is not picked up by the hawk, being knocked unconscious for several minutes in the snow will leave it wet and dangerously cold. Should this occur, pick it up immediately and place it on a dry towel in a cardboard box in a warm and quiet spot. Recovery takes up to a few hours, after which the bird should be released. If the incident occurs at the end of the day, the bird should be kept overnight. Not all birds will recover, but it is amazing how many do!

Providing natural food sources

Birds are often attracted to an area that has the possibility of providing a natural food source. Native plants and trees that offer berries and fruit as well as shelter will attract a greater number and wider variety of birds. Pine and spruce, as well as native tall grasses and meadow plants such as goldenrod, asters, sunflowers, and bergamot, provide seeds and habitat for birds in all seasons of the year. Other plants favored by many seed- and berry-eating birds are native shrubs such as dogwoods, viburnum, staghorn sumac, and evergreens. Plants with tubular flowers such as beardtongue, touch-me-not, and honeysuckle will attract hummingbirds. Avoid non-native species such as Russian olive or barberry. Although attractive to some species of birds, these plants are invasive and will quickly spread to natural areas through bird droppings.

Selecting bird seed

Birds have a variety of food preferences and you will be amply rewarded by paying attention to these. Silo-type feeders of niger and millet will reward you with finches and winter sparrows. Multiple-bin feeders filled with peanut halves, sunflower seeds and cracked corn will attract jays, nuthatches, cardinals, and chickadees. Woodpeckers prefer suet hung on a tree trunk. Orioles prefer orange halves, while some species will eat dried fruit or apple slices. Hummingbird feeders require a solution

To attract a greater diversity of birds, provide a variety of foods and feeders. Shown here are American goldfinches at a silo-type niger feeder, a waxwing enjoying a crabapple feast, and a multi-hopper feeder that offers different seed mixes.

Peter Rasberry

Edward Cheskey

Edward Cheskey

Attracting Wildlife

of four parts boiled water to one part sugar. (This will begin to ferment, with predictable consequences, after a few days, so change the water mixture regularly!)

If you have room for only one feeder, a mixed seed may be your best buy. Prices vary for many reasons, but the most important is the quality of the feed. More expensive mixes contain a higher percentage of nutritious and desirable seed and less "filler" such as wheat which few species will eat. Try limiting mixed-seed feeding to one feeder while providing specific seeds in a number of other feeders. If you feed peanuts or sunflower seeds, do not buy salted seed; and do not feed bread crumbs which have little nutritional value and swell when wet. Be prepared to feed the birds just before and during storms and periods of extreme cold when the risk of starvation is greatest. Regular maintenance of feeders (topping up, cleaning after rainy weather) can become a valued routine for your class and instill a sense of responsibility and stewardship. Cleaning up can also save birds' lives, as toxic molds are known to grow in old seed.

Keep in mind that feeders can encourage and support some species that cause problems for songbirds, such as jays, cowbirds, and squirrels. Jays are nest predators, while cowbirds are nest parasites who lay their eggs in the nests of other birds, often to the detriment of the offspring of their "hosts." Baby cowbirds hatch earlier and grow faster, and their presence in the nest sometimes results in the undernourishment or death of the host's nestlings. Cowbird parasitism is linked to the decline of several species of forest songbirds in eastern North America. Squirrels, whose populations have been inflated by the presence of bird feeders and other aspects of the urban environment, have been implicated in increased levels of nest predation of open-cup nesting birds in urban forests. If you decide to feed peanuts and sunflower seeds, be aware that squirrels are especially attracted to these. Place the feeder on a smooth metal pole which is not directly under a tree. The addition of a cone-shaped baffle may further deter this determined, quick-witted nest predator. Controlling types of feed, squirrel-proofing feeders, and keeping abreast of the latest methods of discouraging these species should allow you to continue enjoying feeding birds without feeling guilty.

Getting your feeders up early (September through November) helps to set a pattern for the birds, but don't fret if you are late. Many birds are quite transient in their small flocks. We often have half a dozen American goldfinches at our feeder. If we band all six one day, we usually find a different, unbanded six the next day! Birds which are not as transient know their home areas well, and if you put out a new feeder in their territory they will be around to check it out. You can continue feeding after cold weather departs, but choose seed carefully to avoid supporting cowbirds: put out smaller seed such as niger and millet rather than cracked corn and sunflower seeds.

Peter Rasberry

Attracting birds to your schoolyard will almost certainly generate curiosity and enjoyment among students. An interest in birds can also become the basis of projects that extend students' experience to community action and scientific research.

Providing water

While many species of birds obtain most of the water they need from their food, a water feature will unquestionably increase the diversity and abundance of birds visiting your site. A simple birdbath works well but does require occasional cleaning, as water that is fouled with bird feces can become a source of disease. Moving water is more likely to attract birds' attention than still water. An effective and inexpensive way of creating movement is to set up a drip from a large jug suspended over a puddle or birdbath.

Linking to the curriculum

Attracting birds to your schoolyard will almost certainly generate curiosity and enjoyment among students. An interest in birds can also become the basis of projects that extend students' experience to community action and scientific research. Take stock of what your community offers. Is there a nearby forest or ravine that would afford a quiet study area for a class if feeders and log benches were installed? Look at the local stream to see what opportunities it presents for creating good bird habitat. A partnership between your school and the local parks department may be a good way to show students that they are part of a larger environment which they can influence through positive community action.

The behavior of birds at feeders fascinates young and old alike and can lead to interesting and thought-provoking questions for student researchers to pursue: Which species is the bossiest? Are some individuals within a species bossier than others? Does the saying "birds of a feather flock together" actually apply to birds? Students can also contribute to current research through participation in Project FeederWatch, an international study to monitor winter bird populations across North America. The program develops primary research and observation skills by requiring participants to identify species, record feeding dates and frequencies, and research the behavior (competition/cooperation, courtship, maintenance, pecking orders, migrations) of individual species. It is also quite desirable to have parents help students gather data at a home feeder, as this will foster a positive communication between family members.

The monitoring of birds' feeding behavior, distribution and abundance is an opportunity for students to develop skill in many mathematical processes. From data gathered while watching a feeder over a period of time, students can calculate frequencies, ratios and proportions, present data graphically, and predict and correlate their observations with other variables such as weather and disturbance.

Another way of bringing a new dimension to your bird studies is to involve bird banders who mark and release wild birds as a means of helping ornithologists discover migration patterns and longevity of species, among other things. Banding is regulated in Canada and the United States, where almost all birds are protected in law from being caught or harmed. A provincial or state banding association may be able to put you in touch with banders who are willing to work with schools. Banding requires capturing and handling birds. During this process, students may have opportunities to view birds up close, listen to their heartbeats, and experience birds in special ways.

Planning a habitat restoration area to attract birds can be time-consuming and challenging, but in the end it is more than worth the effort. Beatrix Potter, a Victorian naturalist best known for her children's books, said, "The only lasting peacefulness is Nature, and it would be well if children — old and young — would study it...." Inviting birds to your school will help you to achieve Potter's vision. ❧

Ken Quanz is a science teacher at Stanley Park Public School in Kitchener, Ontario. Edward Cheskey is a bird conservation planner with the Federation of Ontario Naturalists in Guelph, Ontario.

Gail Littlejohn

Watching a bird bander at work introduces students to methods of scientific data-gathering and offers the opportunity to view birds up close.

Resources

Cornell Lab of Ornithology (http://www.ornith.cornell.edu): Sponsor of bird-monitoring projects such as Project FeederWatch, Classroom FeederWatch, and Nest Box Network, through which students can contribute to scientific research. Educational resources include an online magazine called *Birdscope* filled with stories, illustrations, and student activities that follow the Classroom FeederWatch protocol; and a series of resources developed through BirdSource (http://www.birdsource.com). Contact Cornell Lab of Ornithology, 159 Sapsucker Woods Road, Ithaca, NY 14850-1999. In Canada, Project FeederWatch is sponsored by Bird Studies Canada, PO Box 160, Port Rowan, ON, N0E 1M0, http://www.bsc-eoc.org/pfw.html.

Journey North (http://www.learner.org/jnorth/): An online education initiative through which students track the northward progress of spring, entering data on first sightings of birds and other animals and the first blooms of plants.

Partners in Flight (http://www.PartnersInFlight.org): An international coalition of organizations working to reverse population declines in migratory birds. Click on "Educational Resources" at the web site.

Projects for the Birds

Build a foolproof nesting box

Mounting nesting boxes is an excellent way to boost schoolyard bird populations. This structure accommodates chickadees, swallows, bluebirds, titmice, wrens, and nuthatches. Invasive starlings are excluded because of the size of the entrance.

1. Start with two pine boards: 1 x 6 x 28.5" and 1 x 5 x 22".

2. Cut each board into three panels: the longer, 7.5" (top), 9" (front), and 12" (back); the shorter, 4" (bottom) and two 9" sides.

3. Assemble the panels using 2" coated flat-head screws.

4. Drill a 1.5" entrance hole 1" from the top of the front panel.

5. Drill a few drainage holes near the walls in the bottom panel and a few ventilation holes near the top of each side.

6. Mount the box 6-10 feet off the ground.

7. Unscrew one panel and clean out nesting materials each fall.

by Steven Uriarte

Top: Building birdhouses at a workbee at St. Matthew School in Regina, Saskatchewan. Bottom: A pileated woodpecker enjoys what a handmade feeder has to offer.

Give wildlife an edge

Many wild creatures love to "live on the edge." They flourish in borderline areas where two or more habitats meet. Here's how to create such focal points of productivity in your schoolyard:

❧ Copy nature by arranging native plants in a way that mirrors the transition from, say, woodlands to grasslands or marshes to meadows.

❧ Encircle trees with shrubs or climbing vines, followed by wildflowers and tall grasses, and, finally, open spaces with shorter grasses, ground cover, or lawn. Such arrangements provide different levels of habitat for different wildlife species: those that prefer high tree canopies, those that seek middle levels, and those that feed on the ground.

❧ Provide plant diversity. Include a wide variety of native trees, shrubs, vines, legumes, perennial wildflowers, annual wildflowers, ground covers, and native grasses to meet the needs of diverse species.

❧ Make the most of even the smallest space by planting edges just at the perimeter of your schoolyard.

Plant food sources

Nourish schoolyard wildlife throughout the year by planting a banquet of edibles. Be sure to choose plants, trees, and shrubs that are native to your ecozone.

❧ Canada plum, elderberry, thimbleberry, prickly gooseberry, raspberry, and serviceberry provide spring and summer fruits for a wide variety of wildlife species.

❧ Entice hummingbirds by planting day lilies, fireweed, wild geraniums, phlox, and delphiniums, or by training vines onto arbors or trellises with brightly colored trumpet- or tube-shaped flowers such as honeysuckle and scarlet runner bean.

❧ Autumn is the time when birds store up energy to survive the long flight south or the frigid winter. Offer fall foodstuffs with fruit-bearing shrubs such as red osier dogwood, American mountain ash, buffalo berry, and chokecherry.

❧ The most important food plants are ones whose seeds and fruit last through winter to early spring when food is hardest to find. Provide vital nourishment with highbush cranberry, bittersweet, hawthorn, wild crabapple, white spruce, staghorn sumac, beech, Manitoba maple, black walnut, and American chestnut.

Mud holes and ponds bring new visitors to the schoolyard.

Make waves for wildlife

Introducing water to your schoolyard can have an amazing "ripple effect," benefiting a whole web of species:

❧ Build a pond. A shallow pool in a partially shaded corner will entice birds to drink and frolic.

❧ Offer a birdbath. An unparalleled attraction for a wide assortment of wildlife visitors, its basin should slope towards the middle and be no deeper than 6 cm (2.5"). Add fresh water daily and clean once a week.

❧ Make a splash. A sure way to tantalize wildlife is with tumbling water. It could be as humble as a leaky faucet dripping into a trash can lid or as showy as a waterfall cascading into a luxuriant pool.

❧ Maintain a mud hole. Phoebes, thrushes, and swallows need mud to build their nests in late spring and summer. Create a mud hole by mixing clay soil with water. Maintain it with a regular sprinkling of water. ❦

Steven Uriarte is a writer and editor with the Canadian Wildlife Federation in Ottawa, Ontario.

For information on wildlife food plants indigenous to your ecozone, visit www.wildaboutgardening.org.

Attracting Wildlife

Butterfly Gardens

I f by chance you are one of those admirable people who has decided you are done talking and will now Do Something for our environment, perhaps even more specifically for the environment of children, then you may wish to consider creating a butterfly garden on your school grounds. For now, disregard that by doing so you'll be helping these whimsical insects. Never mind that support will come quite easily because students, parents, and teachers alike will be charmed by your proposal. Don't even be swayed by garden recipes calling for certain trees which will happily serve double duty as shade makers. Ignore how pretty it will be and how sweet it will smell and how many others like hummingbirds, bees, spiders, song birds, and reptiles will joyfully partake of the garden's bounty, drawing you on to connect with the whole wide world. Even overlook the pride and knowledge that will flutter into your school community. Just do it because it's fun!

by Kim Denman

Selecting a site

So how is it done? Quite simply, butterfly gardens are shaped by the needs of butterflies themselves. While some of these needs vary among species, others are common to all. You should start by selecting a location that receives at least six hours of full sunlight per day and is not exposed to excessive wind. Being cold-blooded, butterflies must absorb heat until they have warmed sufficiently for flight. Gravel paths, large flat rocks, or nearby evergreens absorb heat and provide ideal spots for basking. An area of shrubs with leaf litter or trees will provide niches for the butterflies to shelter in.

For the health of your plants, a well drained site is important, but moisture must be available too because many butterflies engage in "puddling," a feeding activity whereby they gather on damp places to absorb essential minerals, particularly sodium. If you don't have a persistent puddle or seep present, you may be able to create one, or you can fill a bucket almost to the rim with sandy soil, submerge it in the ground, keep it moist, and place a few perching twigs or rocks on its surface. If you choose to use wood for structures such as steps or retaining walls, be certain that it is untreated. Toxins in treated woods leach into the soil and can be absorbed by the plants the butterflies will feed on.

Harold Reesor

It's easy to get support for a project aimed at helping such whimsical creatures.

Choosing plants

There are a number of things to consider when choosing nectar flowers. Butterflies are attracted to certain colors, and the ease with which nectar can be extracted through the proboscis is also critical. Butterflies generally have a passion for purples

Greening School Grounds

77

and are also attracted to bright shades of red, yellow, and orange. Single bloomers and flowers with flat tops such as black-eyed Susan, cosmos, and aster, or flowers with short tubes such as lupine, all have accessible nectar. Tough, drought-resistant perennials which successively span a lengthy bloom time should be favored while any non-native invasive flowers should be avoided.

There are no generalizations to be made for larval food plants. Caterpillars are very particular to their host plant, although more than ten species of butterflies do lay their eggs on either trembling (quaking) aspen or cottonwood. Still, monarchs are particular to milkweed, red admirals to nettles, and some swallowtails to willow. Still others fancy certain grasses or thistles, and on it goes. And you thought kids were fussy!

To match leaf to mandible, you will need to determine which butterflies inhabit your region. Consult books, the Internet, and your local naturalists' society. Naturalists may be able to provide you with a list of local butterflies and perhaps even direct you to a nearby butterfly garden for a first-hand look at desirable plants. Once you know exactly which butterflies to expect in your garden, you will be able to select the larval food plants. A final consideration on plant selection is to avoid any that produce toxic fruit; check your plant book or contact your poison control center about any dubious plants.

If your plant list grows too long and begins to seem overwhelming, it is feasible to tailor your garden to the needs of only a few butterflies, perhaps those now locally endangered. You can always plan for a second phase to be undertaken at that idyllic time in the future when you'll be ready to cater to all caterpillars. Of course the ultimate option is to incorporate the butterfly garden into a larger naturalization plan, using it as the catalyst to create an ever-expanding oasis of nature.

Obtaining plants

Once you've created your plant list, you may find that obtaining native plants presents some difficulties. Some garden centers do offer natives for sale, but ascertain that these are nursery grown rather than collected from the wild. If you find, as we did, that you must buy from a wholesaler to obtain some of the plants, be aware that they can sell out of stock well in advance of spring and often have minimum order requirements. We were able to increase our wholesale order to the minimum and raise funds at the same time by offering a plant sale to the community. This had the added benefits of providing an opportunity for others to purchase native species, community education, and increased distribution of these plants in gardens throughout the neighborhood. We also grew many flowers and larval food plants from seed, both perennials and annuals; this was cost effective and we avoided nursery grown plants which are usually sprayed with pesticides.

Designing and planting your garden

Prepare the garden site by removing any unwanted plant life and digging in a generous amount of garden-mix topsoil. Plan the layout considering perimeters, paths or stepping stones for access, and placement of the plants. Design the garden so that taller plants are at the back, or in the center if you are planting an "island." It is also advisable to group smaller plants of the same variety so that they grow to form clumps, making a bolder visual splash for attracting wayward butterflies. You may decide to work in stages, planting trees and shrubs in the fall followed by the flowers in the spring. Just prior to our big planting day, we found it helpful to place labels for each of our plants in the garden, then mark their location on a sketch. Even though someone had fun switching a few of these labels around the night before, our sketch helped us to set things right and volunteers easily found the proper spot for each plant.

Karen Oberhauser

To match leaf to mandible, you will need to determine which butterflies inhabit your region.

Once your garden is planted, you can add to its appeal on special occasions by providing tasty trays of rotting fruit; some butterflies like this. If shelter is lacking, you can purchase or build butterfly boxes for this purpose. (Check a nature supply shop.)

We completed our project by putting together an album that included pictures, a newspaper article about our garden, a map, and other related information that had accumulated. The album is available for reference — and for showing off!

Maintaining the garden

The last hurdle to clear is maintenance. Adding a generous layer of organic mulch (not bark mulch) is a wonderful method of keeping down weeds and preserving moisture, although weeding and watering must still be attended to. We were fortunate in having 20 parents volunteer to water the garden through the first summer, enough so that each had to do this only once to provide the garden with a twice weekly watering. Maintenance for the first two or three years will be more intensive than in future when the plants will have established themselves, but be aware this is an ongoing concern and one of the biggest stumbling blocks to any greening project. Wouldn't it be great if school districts could be convinced to take this on with all the gusto they give to grass cutting?

As for me, I have a confession to make. My involvement in our school's butterfly garden project was the repayment of a long overdue debt. The first time I saw what I now know was a swallowtail caterpillar, it was dangling from the lips of my seven-month-old son. I shrieked hideously, yanked the poor creature from my startled son's gums and flung it across our yard. The fact that this smooth-skinned, many-footed, horned, and fakely bespectacled thing had been in my baby's mouth was so revolting, I never stopped to consider the poor caterpillar. Distasteful as the experience was (for me; I can't speak for my son), I would be much more reasonable the next time. I would gently reprimand my son for trying to eat the poor creature, and I'd tenderly place the caterpillar on a willow leaf. After all, I've come to know caterpillars and treasure them, and I believe that through the garden we planted, others learned this too.

Above: A butterfly box. Below: Monarch butterflies raised in the classroom are released on a butterfly bush at Crestview Public School, Kitchener, Ontario.

By the way, if you bought that line about doing all of this just for fun, by now you are quite likely harboring the dark suspicion that it also involves considerable work. So allow me to simply wish you joy in the endeavor. ❧

Kim Denman is a writer in Surrey, British Columbia, where she assisted with the butterfly garden at Hyland Elementary School.

Gary Pennington

Site Enhancements and Safety

🍂 **Benches, Bridges and Other Beautiful Things** by Gary Pennington

🍂 **Sun Shelters: Respite from the Rays** by Drew Monkman

🍂 **Schoolyard Ponds: Safety and Liability** by Sharon Gamson Danks

🍂 **Discouraging Vandalism in Schoolyard Habitats** by Beth Stout

🍂 **Composting at School** by Rhea Dawn Mahar

Benches, Bridges and Other Beautiful Things

by Gary Pennington

or school grounds to be true learning grounds, they must be rich in diversity and full of potential for exploration and discovery, which are at the heart of learning. Natural areas such as gardens and habitats for wildlife are important elements in this diversity, but so too are the structures and walkways that constitute the built environment of the grounds. Benches, tables, boardwalks and other furnishings not only increase the usefulness of the school grounds as an outdoor classroom; they also make the area more inviting, interesting, and aesthetically pleasing to students and community. Including a variety of built structures in your schoolyard design will have the additional benefit of creating opportunities for artistic and "handy" parents to contribute to the project, and for students to enjoy hands-on but guided practice with the tools and methods of woodworking, metalworking and other crafts.

The scope for site enhancement is enormous and limited only by imagination and the time and energy devoted to seeing dreams become a reality. The following practical advice focuses on a few of the many site enhancements that might be undertaken in a schoolyard.

Benches and tables

Students need places to sit, rest, eat, study, and gather in small groups for social and educational purposes. While a variety of benches and tables can serve this need, there are a few design guidelines which will help to ensure that your structures are appropriate for the school grounds:

Bench encircling a tree provides a shelter in the shade.

❧ Benches and tables should be constructed to weather the elements and to stand up to heavy use and the possibility of vandalism. Rather than using standard-dimension lumber, it is advisable to build with full two-inch or three-inch thick planks that have a minimum width of six inches. Heavier timbers have much greater aesthetic appeal and will reduce maintenance and repair in the long term.

❧ All hardware should be galvanized and joinery should be done with heavy nuts, bolts, and screws rather than with nails.

❧ Do not use pressure-treated wood in the construction of benches, tables, handrails, or any other structures where hands are in frequent contact with surfaces. Instead, select untreated lumber and apply a good protective finish that is certified as non-toxic.

❧ Consider scaling benches and tables to the different sizes of the children and adults who will use them, and ensure that all resting areas are accessible to people with special needs.

Another way of providing for seating is to use large boulders or tree roots for this purpose. If you have ready access to a beach or lake, you can create marvelous resting places with pieces of driftwood. Where large natural objects are used for seating and other purposes, they should be carefully selected and placed so that no sharp edges are in evidence and there are no cavities where children could become entrapped between rocks or logs. Rather than bringing large objects to the site and placing them when students are not around, give students a large say in the way things are arranged; they will relish the opportunity to do so and it will increase their excitement and sense of ownership.

Bridges

Bridges are not only utilitarian but also hold great intrigue for youngsters. (Whether trolls really live under certain bridges is still an open question.) Bridges need not be over watercourses: they can span hills, dry gulches, or even small depressions in a grassy lawn. Small bridges no longer than a few feet will satisfy the needs of young children, while more challenging structures such as rope and Burma bridges can be created with older students. Moreover, a bridge can be a thing of beauty and have a variety of uses. A bridge built for the Children's Garden at the University of British Colum-

bia was called Marble Drop Bridge because visitors can drop a marble down through a post and see it shine among thousands of other marbles in the small stream it overlooks. This is the kind of magical element that transforms a structure from something to pass over to something that increases what Rachel Carson termed "our sense of awe and wonder."

Bridge construction is actually quite simple and the kinds of bridges normally seen on a playground do not require an engineer's stamp, although they must be sturdy and safe. Strong girders, or horizontal support beams made of heavy timbers, are the most common structural element. Girders should be pressure-treated to prevent rot. Heavy planking of either treated lumber or wood such as cedar provides a good walking surface for the bridge. The width of a bridge should be at least 1.2 meters (48") to allow easy passage of wheelchairs; and the height of hand-rails should conform to building code requirements, normally 1.05 meters (42"). Vertical barriers must also conform to code with spacing between uprights not exceeding 10 cm (4"). All walking surfaces should have a finish that is slip-resistant under both wet and dry conditions. The surface treatments used by marina owners to ensure the safety of their patrons may be appropriate for school bridges.

Top: Curved paths at Scarfe Children's Garden, University of British Columbia. Bottom: Father and daughter at work on a schoolyard bridge in Adelaide, Australia.

Boardwalks and pathways

Boardwalks were first used by pioneers as early sidewalks which enabled them to stay clear of the muck and mud of unpaved streets. They still exist in some rural communities and in heritage sites around the continent. Walking on a boardwalk is inherently engaging, and boardwalks make interesting surrounds to ponds and other water areas. They also allow wheelchair access to areas that would not otherwise be accessible. For the most part, the notes to do with bridge building in the previous section apply to boardwalks. Spacing between boards should be large enough to permit drainage of surface water and yet no wider than 1.2 cm (1/2") so as not to catch the heels of shoes.

Paths and nature trails

Paths are a close cousin to the boardwalk. They allow people to get to various parts of the site without interfering with ongoing activities, and they can be venues for many interesting activities. For instance, some schools create nature trails that serve as footpaths for much of the year but become cross-country ski trails in winter. There are a number of basic considerations and requirements in the design of pathways and nature trails:

⚘ Wherever possible, trails should follow old footpaths and take advantage of attractive land features.

⚘ The beginning of the trail should be easily accessible, and the grade and elevation variability should be moderate.

⚘ Trails and paths must be well drained to ensure usability and to reduce maintenance. This can be done by elevating paths to a height of 5-10 cm (2"-4") above grade and infilling where necessary.

⚘ Paths should be from two to three meters (6'-10') wide to facilitate the passage of people in wheelchairs, of two people walking or running abreast, and, in northern regions, cross-country skiers.

⚘ Surfaces must be firm enough to allow for wheeled access and safe use by the elderly as well as the very young. An 8 cm (3") layer of compacted crusher dust on top of a more porous road base works well.

⚘ Consider lighting to provide safe passage, to reduce vandalism, and to increase usage.

⚘ Design pull-off points with benches and tables as part of the path network.

Driftwood and large boulders create informal resting places and private vantage points on a nature trail at West Bay School in West Vancouver.

The borders of trails and pathways should be rich and varied. The late west coast artist Sam Black once wrote with respect to the planned University of British Columbia Children's Garden: "Please not only consider color and variety in plants but also texture and scented plants for sighted as well as blind people. Include sculpted forms to touch and move into and onto. Encourage color walks, texture walks, etc. Encourage explorations of natural materials — wood, clay, sand, water, etc." The insight that Black provides should be a hallmark of our work with pathways and other childhood domains at school and home. As the saying goes, we need to find time to smell the roses, and they need to be there if we are to do so. The byways on our pathways are just as vital as the paths themselves.

One final but important note about pathways: Do not make them straight! Roads, driveways, trails and pathways need to have curves and changes in them to be inviting. Dorothy's yellow brick road would neither look right nor feel right if it were a straight line. Little in the natural world is constructed in this way. To complement rather than compete with nature, we need to use soft curves rather than sharp lines in the ways we enhance the environment. Make winding paths!

Birdhouses and bird feeders

The construction of birdhouses and feeders is well within the skill level of elementary school students and offers opportunity for real accomplishment in welcoming wildlife to the schoolyard. Books on building birdhouses and feeders are readily available at most libraries, and materials to construct them are easily obtained and inexpensive. In fact, birdhouses are so small that most of the wood needed to build them can be found in the scrap heaps of lumber yards or gathered for free from homes and businesses around the community. This approach provides a graphic example to young people of the three "Rs" that educators are trying to inculcate.

Site Enhancements and Safety

Birdhouses and feeders should be situated in places where they are unlikely to be vandalized and yet remain accessible for cleaning and refilling. Often this is just outside upper-story school windows. Where this is done, special supervisory care must be taken to ensure safe access for maintenance. Birdhouses should not be placed in the direct sunlight because of the intense heat that can be generated inside of them. In addition, builders should be encouraged to construct houses that have a natural look, such as through the introduction of branches and twigs to the outside of houses.

Attempting to improve the land around us for educational and social purposes is both a privilege and a challenge. The outdoor world that children and youth face each day at school is often gray, dangerous and uninviting. But as we look around at our many degraded landscapes, we cannot indulge ourselves in collective hand-wringing; rather, our job is to work with young people to transform this reality into special places where learning and caring can flourish. ✿

Gary Pennington is an Emeritus Professor at the University of British Columbia and a play and playgrounds advocate who works with people to naturalize and enhance school grounds.

Gary Pennington

"St. Matthew Secret Garden: A special place to rest, talk with a friend, dream, listen to birdsong, look for tadpoles, watch butterflies & ladybugs, worship, read, learn about nature, write poetry, smell the flowers, leave small gifts. To rediscover our sense of wonder & show that we care for the environment."

Sun Shelters:
Respite from the Rays

by Drew Monkman

The sun shelter is a defined teaching space for outdoor lessons and a popular retreat during recess.

The success of school grounds projects in creating near-at-hand outdoor classrooms and valuable wildlife habitat has come at a time when the health risks associated with being outdoors during peak hours of sunlight are at an all-time high. With medical studies showing increases in UV-related conditions such as skin cancer and eye damage, how is it possible for teachers and students to make full use of their school's natural habitat area? A partial solution to this challenge is to provide comfortable shade and seating in the form of a permanent sun shelter.

Our school's sun shelter is an A-frame, post-and-beam structure that measures approximately 21 feet by 21 feet (6.5 x 6.5 m). It was built by a team of parent and teacher volunteers over the course of two weekends in 1996 for a cost of about $2,000 Canadian ($1,450 U.S.). Four six-inch by six-inch columns on each side are anchored four feet in the ground with limestone screenings. The roof, covered in green sheet metal, slopes from seven feet above ground level at its lowest point to ten feet above ground at its highest. Seven-foot sections of old utility poles were cut in half lengthwise to provide bench seating for about 50 students on the shelter's grass floor. The structure was made of pressure-treated lumber; however, given the problem of toxicity that has been identified with this wood, we would today choose an untreated but rot-resistant wood such as white cedar.

The shelter has proven very popular with students, especially those who do not wish to play sports or go on the climbers. In the past, the only option for these children has been to wander around the schoolyard until the bell rings. At every recess during spring and fall, groups of friends head to the shelter to sit and talk, play, and even draw or do homework.

The structure has also encouraged greater use of the adjacent habitat area. Many classes start their visit by gathering in the shelter to review the purpose of the outing and any special instructions, and finish by returning to the shelter to complete work sheets or discuss what they have learned. The structure creates a defined teaching space where students can concentrate with less distraction, and some teachers report a greater sense of class control — an important point since fear of lack of control is one reason why many teachers hesitate to take their students outside. Finally, because the sun shelter has enough seating for two classes, teachers have the option of going outdoors with a "buddy" class, thereby benefitting from the support of a second teacher. ⓢ

Drew Monkman teaches grades three and four at Edmison Heights Public School in Peterborough, Ontario.

Schoolyard Ponds: Safety and Liability

by Sharon Gamson Danks

Engaging, attractive schoolyard ponds provide habitat for wildlife and hold great educational promise, affording opportunities for students to take "field trips" without leaving the school campus. At the same time, ponds pose safety and liability concerns for schools. Although students can be instructed to behave responsibly around ponds, accidents can happen, and schools have legitimate concerns about the risk of students drowning or the danger of neighborhood children playing alone in the schoolyard after hours. In some regions there is an additional concern about the spread of disease by mosquitoes, and about simpler problems such as the mud students may get on their clothes or track into the building.

Fears about water safety and the liability issues they present can lead school districts and municipalities to impose strict guidelines on pond construction. Such guidelines vary greatly throughout North America. Some districts require metal grates across the surface of the water, tall locked fences around the water body, or other structural solutions that are unattractive and make the pond less accessible to the students and wildlife it was built for. Other authorities simply restrict the depth of the water or the size and location of the pond. Before building a pond, it is important to ensure that your project complies with the guidelines set by your school, school district, or municipality. At the same time, be prepared to think creatively about how you can meet safety requirements while still making your project worthwhile.

Pond advocates take a variety of approaches in addressing these issues. First, mud is a relatively easy concern to respond to. At some schools, students wear rubber wading boots to protect their clothing during class visits to the pond. One elementary school in Colorado has reduced mud problems by restricting access to their popular pond through the use of recess "pond passes" in the form of brightly colored, tee-shirt-like pinafores. Each classroom has five pinafores and rotates their use among the children who wish to play near the pond during recess. This effective solution means that the pond's floating boardwalks are less crowded and the children are less likely to fall into the shallow water and get muddy. Children who do get muddy on a regular basis are required to keep a change of clothes at school.

Stagnant pond water can be home to breeding mosquitoes which in some parts of North America can carry diseases such as encephalitis. Mechanical pond circulation systems run by solar panels (which offer additional educational value) are one solution to this problem because mosquitoes prefer not to lay their eggs in moving water. Another option is to stock the pond with mosquito-eating fish that are indigenous to your geographic location. Provide the fish with sturdy underwater hiding places such as open-ended lengths of pipe to protect them from raccoons and other predators.

No gates, no grates: a safe place to teach water safety

Sharon Danks

THIS 25 CM DEEP (10") WETLAND HABITAT AT an elementary school in Colorado is fenced but not gated or grated, thus allowing children and wildlife free access to the water at all times. Rather than regarding the shallow water as a safety hazard, the school administrators encourage teachers to use it as an opportunity to instruct students in safe behavior near open bodies of water. In an area where there are many swiftly-flowing creeks accessible to the public, they believe that the safety lessons taught at the school pond will help to prevent accidents in local creeks. During the more than ten years that the wetland has been in place, there have been no significant safety problems.

Be prepared to think creatively about how you can meet safety requirements while still making your project worthwhile.

Addressing the risk of drowning usually requires more complex solutions such as the installation of barriers. If your school district absolutely requires the construction of a metal safety grate across the surface of the pond, try to install it several centimeters below the water's surface to make the pond more attractive and functional. In addition, choose a metal grate with openings small enough to prevent a child from falling through but large enough to allow students to take pond samples and to allow small wildlife such as frogs, turtles, and dragonflies to use the water without becoming trapped as they climb in and out.

Another drowning-prevention strategy is to construct the pond inside a closed courtyard at the school, allowing the building itself to serve as the "tall fence" that restricts access. Generally such courtyards are surrounded by windows that will allow students to observe the pond throughout the day. Students can gain access to the pond through the courtyard's doors during class time, and the doors can be locked, if required, at other times of the day. The drawback to locating a pond in an inner courtyard is that you will have to stock it with its initial amphibian inhabitants rather than allowing them to find the pond on their own. Stock the pond with native species, if possible, and if you are planning to remove wildlife from their natural homes, obtain permission to do so.

The ideal location for a schoolyard pond is outside of the school building in an unfenced area that is accessible at all times. This situation most closely mimics natural ponds and is the most attractive and conducive to educational activities and the creation of wildlife habitat. Limiting the pond's depth to less than 30 cm (12") will make it safer and may be enough to assure school and municipal officials concerned about safety and liability. Signage around the pond that explains its purpose and asks visitors to use caution around open water is also important. Low seating walls or simple wooden fences without locked gates are attractive structural devices which will tend to slow down foot traffic, define the pond's boundaries, and keep active games out of the water. All of these measures can help to reduce accidents without denying access to those who want to study the pond more closely. ❧

Sharon Gamson Danks is an environmental planner in San Francisco, California, where she specializes in ecological design and schoolyard naturalization.

Safe, but...

Sharon Danks

IN THIS 45 CM DEEP (18") POND AT A HIGH SCHOOL in California, designers addressed concerns about disease-carrying mosquitoes by installing a solar-powered recirculating pump, and dealt with safety and liability by installing a metal grate over the pond's surface. Unfortunately, a metal grate can itself become a liability: this one admits frogs and dragonflies but is too small to permit passage of most larger wildlife species; it has been repeatedly vandalized by older students who regard its removal as a strength challenge; and its installation above the surface of the water surface significantly detracts from the pond's appearance.

Sharon Danks

Discouraging Vandalism in Schoolyard Habitats

Thoughtful design and community support can help keep your schoolyard off the hit list

Vandalism and the fear of vandalism are major concerns to schools wanting to create or maintain schoolyard habitat sites. In North America, the willful destruction or defacement of property costs schools, homeowners, businesses and others billions of dollars each year. Most vandals are young and the places they vandalize, including schools, are often in the neighborhoods where they live. Yet instances of vandalism to outdoor learning areas are few, and when the sites are designed properly, the threat can be kept to a minimum while students, teachers and community members enjoy a hands-on, outdoor learning opportunity that cannot be duplicated in an indoor classroom setting.

While there is no sure-fire way to prevent vandalism, there are ways to discourage it at your site. The National Crime Prevention Council's "Crime Prevention Through Environmental Design" program focuses on four key strategies, all of which apply in discouraging vandalism at schoolyard habitat sites.

by Beth Stout

Territoriality

People protect territory they feel is their own and have a certain respect for the territory of others. Fences, pavement treatments, art, signs, and good maintenance and landscaping are some physical ways to express ownership. Identifying intruders is much easier in a well-defined space.

Signs

A schoolyard habitat sign should let everyone know that this place is special and why. Just by posting interpretive and other signs, and maintaining them (for example, cleaning off graffiti immediately), you are telling people that this place is used frequently and is monitored and cared for. Incorporate sign design and construction into your habitat project curriculum; it touches on subject areas such as mathematics, art, and language arts.[1]

Maintenance

While schoolyard habitat sites do lessen the need for traditional maintenance, it is still important to keep your habitat area looking presentable to the public. Watering, weeding and general upkeep, especially over the summer, give the impression that your habitat site is being used and enjoyed and that it is not an overgrown weed patch and not an easy target for vandals to attack because no one is watching. Maintaining the habitat site is the responsibility of students, teachers and volunteers. This is a good way to involve neighbors who can lend a hand and keep your

Illustrations: Tom Goldsmith

summer contact person informed about how the site looks and who is using it. To gain the support of neighbors, it is especially important that your site be attractive — not an attractive nuisance!

Location and design

Schoolyard habitat sites can be planned for interior courtyards, fenced-in areas of the schoolyard, or open areas easily accessible to everyone. Where you plan and plant your site depends on the space available and on the steps you can take to discourage vandalism. If your neighborhood has an ongoing vandalism problem, consider an interior courtyard which will limit accessibility. If your school has the funds, fencing might be appropriate for a more open site.

Try developing your site slowly. First, plant a small area and over a period of time add plants and structures such as bird feeders or a water feature. Give everyone a chance to watch the habitat site grow. Work with your students to design your site to be "user friendly" so that there is something for everyone to do when they visit, whether it's a class studying insects, a group of visiting students and teachers who are looking for ideas for their own site, or neighborhood residents who want to sit on a bench and watch the birds. To give as many people as possible a feeling of ownership, hold an open house for the whole school and invite everyone to bring something for the habitat. Whether it's a plant for the butterfly garden, a stone for the path or pond, or a worm for the soil doesn't matter, as long as it connects everyone to the site.

Natural surveillance

Criminals don't want to be seen. Placing physical features, activities, and people in ways that maximize the ability to see what's going on discourages crime. Barriers such as bushes, sheds or shadows make it difficult to observe activity. Landscaping and lighting can be planned to promote natural surveillance both from inside a building and from the outside by neighbors or people passing by. Maximizing the natural surveillance capability of such "gatekeepers" is important.

Landscaping

Involving students in the design of habitat sites is one of the best ways to give them a feeling of ownership and to discourage vandalism. When you and your students are mapping and taking inventory of the site, include human uses of the area. For example, do students currently beat a path across the lawn or through the underbrush; do vandals graffiti the walls; is the area well-lit at night; is it an area that will lend itself to use by the community at large; can neighbors see what's happening at the site? Take the answers to these questions into consideration as you proceed. If walls have a history of attracting graffiti, students can research appropriate vines or shrubs to plant in front of them; if the area is too dark at night, include funds for lighting in your budget; if students have already cut a path through the area, include that path in your site design; and if your site is not in full view of the neighbors, consider moving it so it will be.

Gatekeepers

Most schools require that all visitors stop at the office before going further inside the school. In this sense, the office staff are gatekeepers who keep track of everyone who visits. School neighbors can also act as gatekeepers just by keeping an eye on the habitat site. When visitors are aware that they are being monitored — even informally — it helps to discourage inappropriate behavior. Other ways of "gatekeeping" include keeping a visitors' book at the site; encouraging active use of the site by as many community groups and classes as possible, including classes from other schools; and in the summer encouraging volunteers to maintain a very visible presence by scheduling their activities on various days and at various times of the day, including early morning and evening which are the best times for watering anyway.

Activity Support

Encouraging legitimate activity in public spaces helps to discourage crime. Any activity that gets people out and working together at your habitat site increases community involvement with your project and could lead to unexpected support such as donations of materials or volunteer help. The greater the number of people who are involved with, and care about, your site, the more eyes and ears you will have in the community. Some ideas: hold a community open house; conduct a "bug" count and invite classes from neighboring schools; offer regularly scheduled habitat tours and advertise them in the local paper; hold celebrations in the habitat on special days such as Arbor Day, Earth Day, International Migratory Bird Day and birthdays; develop a mentoring program for your habitat project and reach out to younger students with special activities; hold regular clean-up days to keep up with maintenance and demonstrate that the site is important — for both wildlife and people! Invite high school students to perform service-learning or community service projects.

Access Control

Properly located entrances, exits, fencing, landscaping and lighting can direct both foot and automobile traffic in ways that discourage crime. Another way to maintain access control is to declare the importance of the habitat site to the life of the school by including specific references to it in your school code of conduct and to encourage your school district to include school habitat sites in their policy manuals under "Vandalism" or "Care of School Property by Students." Make sure that everyone understands that vandalism is a crime, that crimes are reported to the police, criminals are prosecuted, and restitution is demanded.

The greater the number of people who are involved with, and care about, your site, the more eyes and ears you will have in the community.

What if we are "hit"?

Despite our best efforts, vandalism is widespread and it can happen to your habitat site. So what do you do if you've been "hit"?

↝ Contact the appropriate authorities. Vandalism is a crime and must be reported to the police. Ask the police to keep an eye on your site as they patrol.

↝ Contact your neighbors. Let them know what has happened and ask if they saw anything you can relay to the police. Ask them to keep a closer watch on the habitat site and make sure they have the phone number of the person to call if they have information.

↝ Clean up immediately! Show the vandals that you will not tolerate their actions and that you will paint over graffiti, replant shrubs, clean up signs, and replace structures such as birdbaths or feeders.

↝ Counsel and continue to educate your students. It can be depressing, even devastating, to be the victim of a crime. Often schools provide grief counselling for students mourning the loss of a classmate or recovering from the tragedy of school violence. Offer your students time and space to express their emotions and concerns about destruction and defacement of a place they worked so hard to create. Students who have been active in the habitat project can visit other classes and schools to talk about what happened and how to prevent it from happening again.

✤ Rethink the design and use of your site. As much as possible, incorporate the four strategies above into the redesign, and always involve students in the design process: their ideas for deterring vandals and involving friends and neighbors are valuable.

✤ Remind yourself of the reasons you planted the habitat site in the first place. Schoolyard habitat sites are outdoor learning areas for students, teachers and members of the community. They provide homes for wildlife; facilitate the study of nature and other subjects; encourage parent involvement; reduce the need for field trips and maximize teaching time; and they are beautiful to look at and enjoyable to be in.

Creating a habitat site on school grounds is one of the most positive contributions you can make to the life of your school and the surrounding community. But creating a place for wildlife right outside the schoolroom door brings with it the responsibilities of stewardship. Vandalism of schoolyard sites, while uncommon, does happen. But don't let the fear of crime deter you; rather, let the joy of creation guide you in taking steps to reduce its frequency and severity. ✤

Beth Stout is the Educational Outreach Coordinator for the National Wildlife Federation in Portland, Oregon. This article was adapted, with permission, from Clearing, *Fall 1999.*

Note

1   Schools in the U.S. that certify a habitat area with National Wildlife Federation are eligible to receive a 19" x 13" aluminum sign designating the school as a certified Schoolyard Habitats site. For information on the NWF Schoolyard Habitats program, visit www.nwf.org.

Composting at School

Composting has a symbiotic fit with any school grounds greening project, but can also play an important educational and ecological role in our schools. By recycling food and yard wastes, we can reduce waste management costs, learn first-hand about decomposition processes, and produce a high-quality soil amendment for school gardens. Yet composting does present challenges: there is no getting around the fact that food waste needs to be collected on a regular basis, usually needs to be carried outdoors, and must be well managed if it is to avoid attracting rodents, exuding odors, and looking unkempt. Composting programs have come and gone over the years, but many schools have created programs that have met the challenges and endured. What these schools have in common is a supportive educational program, school-wide participation, and a consistent maintenance schedule. The following examines these elements and looks briefly at some successful school programs.

by Rhea Dawn Mahar

Elements of success

Foremost among the elements critical to sustaining a composting program is to have a crew of "compost kids" who help to design the system used in the school and who actively and consistently maintain and monitor the program. But students need guidance, permission, coordination and training, much of which must come from keen teachers. Caretakers, too, are crucial and should be consulted and invited to be part of the crew.

Composting programs that are solo operations depending on the interest of only one or a few individuals usually have limited success and little longevity. Instead, what is needed is a school-wide commitment, one that, ideally, is reflected in the school's improvement plan. Another essential is a management plan that includes a schedule of who is collecting and when, and who is turning the outdoor compost pile. Finally, it is both courteous and sensible to seek the permission and advice of your school board's health and safety officer and custodial supervisor. Their comments and support could be very helpful.

Top: Bagging the "pay dirt" at Mt. Sinai School. Bottom: On Friday mornings, the Dufferin School Green Team gets out of class to tend the compost and gardens.

Composting in the curriculum

Teachers can illustrate many lessons and meet many learning outcomes through a school composting program. Almost all curriculum at every grade level encourages hands-on learning, and composting can easily be made the focus of those activities. Here are a few examples:

⟿ To address a grade three science topic such as Exploring Soils, students can analyze the composition and texture of finished compost. For the topic Plant Growth and Changes, they can compare plants grown in soil with and without compost.

⟿ In high school science classes, chemistry students can check the temperature, pH, mass, density, and potassium and nitrogen content of compost at various stages

Mt. Sinai School, Brookhaven, New York

Dufferin School, Winnipeg, Manitoba

Rot Race Challenge

Here's a great exercise to learn more about the composting process.

You'll need:
- 5 one-liter plastic pails with lids
- sifted sterilized potting soil
- compost soil (available at most gardening stores)
- vegetable scraps or fallen leaves
- cutting instrument
- spoon or stick
- newspaper
- alcohol thermometer
- magnifier
- inert objects such as tin foil or plastic

Taking the temperature of the compost.

Instructions:

1. Divide the class into five groups, each of which will test one of the following combinations of materials:
- a) sterilized soil and large vegetable pieces
- b) sterilized soil and finely chopped vegetable pieces
- c) compost soil and large vegetable pieces
- d) compost soil and finely chopped vegetable pieces
- e) compost soil and inert objects

2. Each group should cut a fist-sized hole in the middle of their pail lid to let air in. Label the lid and pail to show which combination of compost you are testing.

3. Fill the pail two-thirds full of the soil type you are using. Then empty the soil onto a piece of newspaper.

4. If you are using finely chopped vegetables, cut them to no bigger than 0.5 cm or 1/4".

5. If using vegetables, mix your finely-chopped or large vegetable pieces with the soil to begin your compost. Examine your soil with the magnifier. Write a description of the soil mixture as it appears now. Then put it in the pail and cover it with the lid. Let the Rot Race begin!

6. Take the temperature of your mixture every day for two weeks, and record it on a chart. Insert the thermometer through the hole in the lid to a depth of two-thirds of the way into the contents.

7. After taking the temperature each day, use the spoon or stick to stir the mixture. Keep the mixture damp by adding some water every second day. Caution: Never use a thermometer to stir the soil mixture.

8. After two weeks, empty your compost combination onto several sheets of newspaper. Compare the soil with how it appeared at the start of the experiment. (The most homogeneous mixture will be "d" since smaller vegetable pieces breakdown more quickly.)

9. Make a graph showing the daily temperatures of your compost combination. (The higher temperatures will be associated with the combination that includes finely-chopped vegetables. The mixture containing inert objects will show no temperature change.)

10. With your classmates, compare the temperatures and the degree of decomposition of each combination. (All but "e" would decompose better if micro-organisms were added. Sterilized soil has few living micro-organisms. In landfills, smaller pieces will break down quickly whereas inert objects will remain intact for a long time.)

An Eco-Team member with an "Organics" collection pail at Shatford Memorial Elementary School.

of decomposition. These measurements are vital diagnostic tools in managing a compost pile. For example, if compost is too cold, it may need more nitrogen and oxygen; if it is releasing odors, it may need more dry leaves or other carbon-rich material.

⤙ Biology students can study the complex web of organisms and interactions that help to create compost.

⤙ In studying waste management, a social studies class can examine how composting reduces the need for landfills and lowers associated waste-management costs.

⤙ Physical education classes can turn the compost on a regular basis to aerate it, and once or twice a year distribute the finished product to planted areas on the school grounds.

⤙ Music students can write lyrics for catchy jingles that will educate other students about composting.

Aside from formal learning opportunities, when students begin to manage their own food wastes they are inevitably drawn into broader learning related to ethics, personal responsibility and environmental citizenship. A sense of personal power emerges as they realize that their food wastes can be easily and quietly turned into nutrients that will improve the soil and ultimately their own health. It is encouraging to learn that the simple act of diverting food scraps from the landfill can help to reduce fossil fuel consumption and habitat destruction.

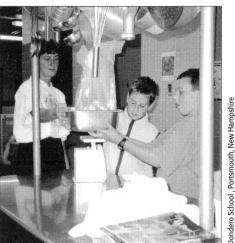

Dondero School, Portsmouth, New Hampshire

Successful school programs

Three methods of composting are presently used in schools. Schoolyard composting is just like residential composting in which buckets of food scraps, mostly fruits and vegetables, are regularly tipped into an outdoor holding bin on the property. Vermicomposting is an indoor system in which food scraps are fed to worms which then transform them into castings rich in nutrients. A lesser-known system currently being adopted by some municipalities is centralized composting in which organic wastes are collected and sent to large compost-processing plants or windrow operations. The following are examples of how schools have devised interesting and successful programs using these different composting methods.

When students begin to manage their own food wastes they are inevitably drawn into broader learning related to ethics, personal responsibility and environmental citizenship.

Schoolyard composting programs

At Dondero School in Portsmouth, New Hampshire, the success of the composting program can be attributed largely to school-wide participation. The Waste to Wonders Committee trains student representatives from each class how to separate food wastes, and these students, in turn, teach their classmates. Every lunch period, student volunteers stand by the compost buckets helping students determine what can be composted. In the kitchen, fifth grade volunteers weigh and chart the organic materials and then tip the compost into the outdoor bin. Once a week, they take the temperature of the compost pile to make sure it maintains the ideal "cooking" temperature (45-65°C/112-150°F).

Some schools support composting by allowing students time off from class to attend to it. At Dufferin School in Winnipeg, Manitoba, Green Team members are excused from class for one hour every Friday morning to collect organic materials from classrooms and to look after outdoor gardens and an indoor hydroponics garden. Since every good compost stew requires moisture, the team periodically pours nutrient-rich liquid from their hydroponics garden over the compost pile to speed up decomposition.

Sometimes it is parents who are the catalysts for school composting. At Mount Sinai School in Brookhaven, New York, Carol and Joe DiLernia translated their enthusiasm for composting into weekly classroom lessons that ranged from discussing technical details to composing musical messages about composting. In the spring, the school's compost pile produces "pay dirt" that is sold at the annual Mother's Day plant sale.

Inviting the expertise and assistance of community organizations can help in creating and maintaining a school program. One of the most continuous rural school composting projects is at Cape Cod Hill School in New Sharon, Maine, where staff of the nearby Woods End Research Laboratory undertook initial training and constructed a compost shed. Three grade six students are on duty every day beside compost barrels in the cafeteria to guide other students in sorting their lunch wastes. The barrels are wheeled out and emptied into bins in the composting shed where "active maintenance" takes place. Food scraps and leaves are added in alternating layers, and the compost is systematically aerated by turning, and occasionally watered. Students monitor air temperature as well as the temperatures inside the compost piles. Every month, the compost piles are turned over. In spring, fully cured compost is worked into the gardens, and any uncured material is brought out to "ripen" outdoors over the summer.

Top: The organics collection team at Colonel John Stuart Elementary is a self-sustaining mix of grade five and six students. Each year, the grade six students teach the grade fives. Bottom: Red wigglers are happy to transform food scraps into nutrient-rich castings.

Vermicomposting programs

Vermicomposting has become popular in many schools, not least because it all takes place in a terrific laundry-hamper-sized worm habitat that fits neatly into any classroom. The cost? The purchase of the initial colony of red wiggler worms and a plastic container. Minimal yet careful management keeps the earthmovers happy and able to do their work of digesting food wastes into rich castings full of nutrients. It sounds simple, but here again, good planning and consistency are the keys to long-term success.

At Michael Wallace School in Dartmouth, Nova Scotia, the student Garden Club, supervised by a parent, is in charge of the school's worm composting program. After attending an initial workshop, wormkeepers devote several days each year to sharing the objectives of their endeavors with fellow students. Teams of club members rotate the daily task of collecting organic wastes from lunchrooms. To reduce the volume of material and make it more immediately digestible by the worms, students grind it a hand-grinder and then freeze it (this breaks down cell walls). Two days later, the thawed, moist, and easily digested material is fed to the worms. Finished vermicompost is dug into outdoor flower beds.

At Olympic Heights School in Calgary, Alberta, students and staff are all committed to the vermicomposting program. There is one worm bin for every two classrooms, and student partners share the associated duties. A Green Committee ensures proper training of students and staff, and articles in the school's newsletter help to maintain the worms' high profile. The vermicomposting program supports grade three and four curriculum units on Animal Life Cycles and Waste in Our World.

Centralized composting programs

In many municipalities across North America, landfills are filling up so quickly that it is no longer feasible to ignore composting opportunities. Nova Scotia is the first province in Canada to achieve 50 percent diversion of solid wastes, and schools there are now required to divert all food wastes. In larger cities such as Halifax, organic wastes are picked up and hauled to central composting plants or to windrow operations where the material is piled in long rows and turned regularly. Working with this system, Eco-team members at Colonel John Stuart Elementary School collect food waste daily from the cafeteria and classrooms and take it to the school's central "Resource Station." The caretaker then transfers it to a large outdoor organics bin from which it is collected weekly. Since the haul-away system began, some schools have stopped schoolyard composting but others maintain on-site programs in order to take advantage of the educational opportunities they provide.

Although composting demands consistent attention, it offers a wealth of hands-on learning possibilities and produces a rich source of soil nutrients for school grounds plantings. Equally important, school composting promotes and demonstrates an ethic of environmental stewardship and personal responsibility. But whether mandated or voluntary, perhaps the best reason to compost at school is just because it's fun. ❧

Rhea Dawn Mahar is an environmental geographer and outdoor classroom specialist in Halifax, Nova Scotia.

Resources

Appelhof, Mary. *Worms Eat My Garbage: How To Set Up and Maintain a Worm Composting System.* Kalamazoo, Michigan: Flower Press, 1982, ISBN 0-942256-03-4.

Marin County Office of Waste Management. *Composting Across the Curriculum: A Teacher's Guide to Composting.* 1993. Department of Public Works, Office of Waste Management, PO Box 4186, San Rafael, CA 94913-4186, (415) 499-6647.

New Hampshire Governor's Recycling Program and New Hampshire Department of Environmental Services. *Composting at New Hampshire Schools: A 'How to' Guide.* 1997. NH Department of Environmental Services, 6 Hazen Drive, Concord, NH 03301, (603) 271-3712.

Payne, Binet. *The Worm Cafe: Mid-Scale Vermicomposting of Lunchroom Wastes.* Kalamazoo, Michigan: Flower Press, 1999, ISBN 0-942256-11-5.

Trautmann, Nancy M. and Marianne Krasny. *Composting in the Classroom: Scientific Inquiry for High School Students.* Kendall/Hunt Publishing, 1998, ISBN 0-7872-4433-3.

For more information about the school programs mentioned in this article, contact:

Dondero Elementary School, New Hampshire (603) 436-2231

Dufferin Elementary School, Manitoba (204) 774-3409

Mount Sinai Elementary School, New York (631) 473-1991

Cape Cod Hill Elementary School, Maine (207) 778-3031

Michael Wallace Elementary School, Nova Scotia (902) 435-8357

Olympic Heights Elementary School, Alberta (403) 777-8370

Colonel John Stuart Elementary School, Nova Scotia (902) 464-5200

Other Nova Scotia schools working with the new centralized composting system:

Holland Road Elementary School (902) 860-4170

Shatford Memorial Elementary School (902) 857-4200

Winter Composting Shelter

SCHOOLS IN NORTHERN AREAS CAN keep their compost cooking all winter using a simple method devised by students at the aptly-named Leslie Frost Public School in Lindsay, Ontario. Concerned because their schoolyard composters could not handle the food scraps of 400 students through the winter, they experimented to find ways to keep decomposition active. They found that a simple shelter surrounding the black plastic composter provided enough insulation to prevent its contents from freezing even in the coldest months.

Constructed of second-hand lumber, clear plastic sheeting, and a few staples, the shelter has a cubic wood frame and double walls of plastic that trap solar radiation and conserve the heat generated by the decomposition going on inside the composter. A hinged lid allows access for adding food scraps, and an indoor-outdoor thermometer enables students to take temperature readings both outdoors and at the center of the compost pile. In contrast to the chilly, dormant world outside, the compost pile stays warm and active all winter.

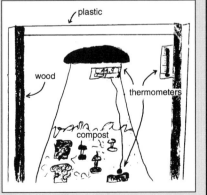

Grade 2 student, Leslie Frost Public School

Felicia Leipzig

Learning in the Outdoor Classroom

🍃 **The Panther Patch: A K-6 Gardening Plan** by Janice Hanscom and Felicia Leipzig

🍃 **Creating a Field Guide to Your Nature Area** by Bruce R. Dean

🍃 **Learning Links for Elementary Classes** by Jeff Reading and George Taven

🍃 **K-12 Activities for the Outdoor Classroom** by Char Bezanson, Craig Johnson, Bill Lindquist and Nalani McCutcheon

🍃 **K-12 Learning in a Schoolyard Prairie** by Robin Greenler

🍃 **The Abundance of Nature's Imagination** by Karen Krupa

🍃 **Math in the Schoolyard** by Char Bezanson and Judy Killion

🍃 **Exploring Food and Culture through Gardening** by Nicole Thibault

🍃 **Tips and Tricks for Taking Kids Outside** by Nalani McCutcheon and Andrea Swanson

🍃 **Service Learning: Connecting Classrooms with Communities** by Mary Haque

The Panther Patch: A K-6 Gardening Plan

by Janice Hanscom and Felicia Leipzig

Children raised in an urban community often miss experiences that develop respect for the land. With this in mind, we have put our time and energy into making sure that the Panther Patch — the garden at our school — is a place where every child may learn not just science but also responsibility for our environment. One of our main aims — and struggles — has been to make gardening a progressive learning experience from kindergarten through sixth grade.

During the first year of our garden, teachers and students grew whatever they wanted. In the second year, we tried having the fourth graders set up experiments to be conducted by students in other grades. But there was no continuity, no sense of each year building on the last: the third grade teacher didn't know what the second grade teacher had planted or what activities the students had already done. In our third year, right after harvest, we talked to the teachers at each grade level to find out what plants, if started the previous spring, could be harvested and integrated into their fall lessons. From these discussions we developed a K to 6 planting plan.

K to 6 gardening progression

In May, kindergarten students plant potatoes in tires that are lined up along the garden fence. The small space helps children of this age know where to plant and allows for better control of the equipment. The following September, as first graders, the students dig the potatoes and use them in a variety of activities. The first grade teachers have a Potato Day on which the children eat potato soup, potato salad, and baked potatoes. The potatoes are also used for printmaking in art projects. In the spring, the first grade students plant wheat seeds.

In September, at the beginning of the second grade, the students go to the garden to collect the wheat. The plants are cut and threshed. Seeds are cleaned, ground, and made into bread. In the spring, second grade students plant marigold seeds. As the seedlings emerge, they are transplanted to the garden to grow around green beans and peas that are seeded directly into the garden bed. In doing the transplanting, students learn about the process of hardening off plants.

The next fall, as third grade students, they harvest seeds from the marigolds, peas, and green beans, and study the structure and development of different seed parts. In March, the students plant many different kinds of everlasting flowers. Learning is focused on seed hitchhikers and how seeds disperse.

As soon as they return to school in the fall the fourth grade students collect flowers and other plant materials to dry. (Over the summer, parents and teachers also collect plants which are added to the students' fall collections.) The dried

Top: The hoop house extends the growing season for squash and pumpkins. Bottom: Raised beds are maintained by students using child-sized tools.

100

Learning in the Outdoor Classroom

flowers are used in arrangements which a local florist helps the students to design after working on the basic concepts of arranging. The flower arrangements are done in coffee mugs and sold during open house at the school. The flowers are also used to study the pollination and seed production of flowers. In May, the students plant the potatoes and onions to be used in fifth grade.

In September, the potatoes and onions are harvested for use in a microscope unit in science. The students make microscope slides of onion cells and have a potato feast. Later, the fifth grade students plant pumpkins in grow carts and then transplant the seedlings into the school's hoop greenhouse in May.

As sixth graders, the students go to the hoop house with the kindergartners (who weren't in school in the spring and thus didn't get to plant anything) to pick the pumpkins. The kindergartners make predictions such as "Which green pumpkin will still turn orange?" and use the pumpkins for activities such as Pin The Nose On The Pumpkin. In the spring, the sixth graders have a sale of the bedding plants they have raised in their grow carts. The money from the sale goes toward the garden. One year the sixth grade donated picnic benches for the grassy area in the garden.

Indoor gardening activities

Since our outdoor gardening season is so short and most of our students do not get to enjoy seeing their plants grow during the summer, we have tried many indoor gardening activities to motivate both teachers and students. These include a variety of activities from the Life Lab curriculum,[1] as well as science units from Wisconsin Fast Plants which use a *Brassica* that matures in 40 days.[2] Sometimes the whole school works on an experiment at the same time; for example, we have designed a series of tests for grades K to 6 to determine how environmental factors affect the germination and growth of lettuce [*see sidebar on next page*]. Students are given complete responsibility for their plants during these studies, and they take this responsibility seriously: one chronically absent first grade student got to school every day during the lettuce experiment to make sure his plant was properly taken care of.

One time we organized an experiment that students did at home. From December to February we have very low light levels and very cold temperatures in Fairbanks, so growing plants is a challenge. That time of year is when "Jack" wrote a letter to all students saying he had heard about their gardening prowess. He had just recently moved to Fairbanks and was looking for help in making his beanstalk grow better. We sent the letter home with students, asking parents if it would be all right to bring home a pot, soil, and seeds to grow. Students who got permission picked up their supplies, took them home, and planted the beans. They kept a journal about their growing experience. Every so often, Jack would send out another cry for help, such as the time he had so many candles going in his cabin that he didn't have enough room to jump over them and wanted to know how the students were providing light for their plants. Once we got a note from Jill. Jack had gone up the hill to get a pail of water, fallen down, and ended up in the hospital. Some students brought him "Get Well" cards with advice on other ways to get water for his plants. In the end they brought their plants back to school, weighed and measured them, and made a huge graph in the hall showing how tall all the plants were. The student with the tallest plant got, of course, a golden egg.

Gardening Timeline

September
- Till the garden and add any soil amendments.
- Establish a gardening committee.
- Identify what each grade will plant.
- Plan teacher training for the year.

October
- Look for funding sources.
- Identify a storage place.
- Check supplies and stock up.

February – March
- Plan for the summer.
- Watch calendar for dates to start seeds indoors.

April
- Put out a planting schedule for sign-up.

May
- Till the garden as soon as possible.
- Assign planting areas for each class.
- Provide teachers with directions for preparing the soil, transplanting outdoors, watering.
- Have a watering schedule in place.

June – August
- Hand over garden care to summer caregivers.
- Build a tool shed.
- Have kids in garden as much as possible.

September
- Harvest the garden first thing before a frost.
- Clean up the garden before snow comes.

Summer care

Caring for a school garden in the summer is a concern everywhere, but especially in the north where the school year and the growing season do not overlap very much. Before starting an outdoor garden, be sure to develop a plan for the summer. It helps to align yourself with as many helpers as possible. One option is to start a junior garden club and join up with a flower or garden club in your community. We dealt with the summer months by starting a 4-H Club because it is a program for both girls and boys and is part of a Cooperative Extension Service which includes Master Gardeners. The 4-H Club members, about half of whom are from other schools, are responsible for caring for the garden all summer. Members who have been involved for several years can apply for an individual garden plot. All maintenance of the garden and its facilities is done by 4-H members, volunteers, and sometimes a paid coordinator if we have received a grant.

Every year we have vandalism. At the suggestion of the students, we built a fence that defines the garden space and keeps kids from running or riding bikes through it. We hope that as children grow with the garden they will take better care of it.

Getting support for your garden

To make a garden work it helps to have the enthusiastic support of the parents, faculty, staff, and administration at the school. The best way to get parents to

---

Lettuce now perform an experiment...

HOW DOES THE ENVIRONMENT AFFECT THE GERMINATION AND GROWTH OF LETTUCE? In this indoor experiment, the testing of environmental factors such as water, light, temperature and nutrients is assigned to different grade levels. Each class writes up their results. The school's combined results can be used the next year as the basis for a contest to see who can use the information to grow the best pot of lettuce. What do you do with all the lettuce? Transplant it to the outdoor garden in spring — or, if you just can't wait, add salad dressing!

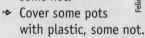
Felicia Leipzig

Grade	Procedure
Kindergarten (4-8 days)	• Start 10 seeds in several pots, possibly soaking some seeds overnight and some not. • Cover some pots with plastic, some not. • Keep all pots equally moist. • Record germination rates for the various treatments.
First grade (3-4 weeks)	• Start 10 seeds in several pots. • Place the pots in different areas of the classroom under various light levels. • Keep all pots equally moist. • Record germination rates and measure the heights of plants at regular intervals.
Second grade (3-4 weeks)	• Start 10 seeds in several pots. • Give each pot a predetermined amount of water at regular intervals. • Record the rates of germination, survival and growth.
Third grade (3-4 weeks)	• Start 10 seeds in several pots. • Place the pots in various places around the room with different temperatures. • Record the temperatures daily. • Record the rates of germination and growth.
Fourth grade (3-4 weeks)	• Start 10 seeds in several pots using different media in each pot. • Water the pots as needed. • Record the rates of germination, survival and growth.
Fifth grade (4-7 weeks)	• Start 10 seeds in several pots. • Water the plants as needed with various concentrations of fertilizer. • Record the rates of germination and growth.
Sixth grade (4-7 weeks)	• Start 10 seeds in several pots. • Apply different kinds of fertilizer in appropriate quantities. • Record the rates of germination and growth.

---

help is to ask them personally. As for teacher support, begin with a consensus from those involved. We suggest starting with a grade level in which gardening fits well in the existing curriculum and expanding from there. A garden program would be difficult without support of the principal. To get the principal interested, you may first need to get the support of the parent-teacher association.

Funders are always looking for innovative science programs, especially in elementary schools. Writing grant proposals is one way to get funding, but you don't need to write proposals to get everything you want. In addition to receiving grants, we have raised money by selling produce from the garden, flower arrangements, and tee-shirts. It is also possible to get donations of materials. Don't limit your requests to a garden store. Try asking the police for supplies such as pots and grow lights taken on drug raids. Think creatively. You just have to find out what is available in your area.

We are now many years into our gardening project and each year we face new challenges and must find new solutions. We've had freezing temperatures after setting out seedlings and thus needed to replant. There have been early frosts before the students have returned to school in the fall. In spite of these trials and tribulations, the project continues as a labor of love. ❧

Felicia Leipzig

Felicia Leipzig teaches fourth grade at Denali Elementary School in Fairbanks, Alaska, and is an avid gardener. Janice Hanscom, whose children attended Denali Elementary, works at the Agricultural and Forestry Experiment Station at the University of Alaska in Fairbanks.

Notes

1 See *The Growing Classroom: Garden-Based Science,* an outdoor gardening curriculum for grades 2 to 6, developed by Life Lab, 1156 High Street, Santa Cruz, CA 95064, (831) 459-2001, www.lifelab.org.

2 Wisconsin Fast Plants, University of Wisconsin-Madison, Department of Plant Pathology, 1630 Linden Drive, Madison, WI 53706, (608) 263-2634, www.fastplants.org.

We talked to the teachers at each grade level to find out what plants, if started the previous spring, could be harvested and integrated into their fall lessons.

The Gardeners' Progress:
A Planting Plan for Kindergarten to Grade Six

Grade Level	Fall Activity	Spring Activity
Kindergarten	See sixth grade	Plant potatoes
First grade	Categorize potatoes, make potato prints	Plant wheat
Second grade	Grind seeds for bread	Plant beans, peas and marigolds
Third grade	Study seeds	Plant flowers for drying
Fourth grade	Make dried flower arrangements	Plant onions
Fifth grade	Study onion cells, microscopy	Plant pumpkins
Sixth grade	Pumpkin activities with kindergarten buddies	Hold a plant sale as a fundraiser for the garden

Creating a Field Guide to Your Nature Area

It's spring... birds chirping, trees budding, ground beginning to thaw. Who wants to stay in a stuffy old classroom? Not me and my students, which is why we're going outside. Over the next six weeks, we'll use our schoolyard as an outdoor classroom, collecting information about the flora and fauna we find. Then we'll use our computer to turn our findings into a field guide to the world of nature around our school. We'll put our technology, art, research, and science skills to work, and have a wonderful time in the process!

May is a perfect time to try a similar project with your students. You'll need a program such as Clarisworks or Microsoft Word and Works, Superpaint or another friendly draw program, colored pencils, fine-tipped markers, pens, clipboards, journals, paper, a specimen jar for collecting insects, magnifiers (page magnifiers work great), a camera, film, and an interest in the ecosystems surrounding your school.

by Bruce R. Dean

Judy Killion

In creating a guide to the schoolyard, students become field researchers always on the lookout for plants, animals, insects and rocks.

The creative challenge

To launch the program, we bring out field guides and show examples from naturalists' sketchbooks, discussing why the guides are useful and important. (This is the time to invite a local naturalist to share methods of recording observations.) We make field sketchbooks out of sheets of blank white paper (bring out those bookbinding lessons — try marbling the covers) and discuss how we'll use them to make notes about and sketch the plants, insects, birds, and other animals we see on the school grounds.

Database design

Next, we show students how to set up a database. We design a standard form for recording our information. Data fields include the common name, scientific name, family, name of discoverer (student's name), date, location, habitat, and unusual features. We set up separate records for the plant, animal, and insect kingdoms, and for geology. Later, the entries can be easily sorted by any database category for introducing approaches to research and for answering questions that are generated as we go. With our database organized, we are ready to go out in the field.

Schoolyard sightings

During class time, lunch, and recesses, students write down in their sketchbooks the names (or descriptions) of all the plants and animals they see on the school grounds. Field samples such as insects, leaves or rocks are sometimes brought indoors and examined under magnification. Using the field guides from our school library, students identify and research their finds and record relevant information in their sketchbooks. Weekly, we input this information into the database. As our database grows, we come to see just how many kinds of flora and fauna are around our school.

Making the guidebook

To assemble our field guide, we first sort the database by families and print it out. We use the printout as an assignment sheet: each student is responsible for writing up one entry for an individual species of animal, bird, insect, or plant, and supplying illustrations for that page of the field guide. As students finish researching, writing, and checking their entries, we format them to fit the field guide's design. At the bottom of each page, we create an empty box in which students can paste pencil drawings, photographs or photocopies. Students with advanced skills may use a computer drawing program to create images for their pages. If you have access to a scanner, hand drawings can be scanned and imported into the students' pages. Have students do their preliminary drawings in pencil and go over them with black ink before photocopying or scanning them. Color can be added afterwards. In June we print out the pages, add the artwork, make a title page, bind our book, and then donate a copy to the school library for other students to use and enjoy. The town library may also be interested in a copy.

Additional activities

Try these hands-on science activities as you work on your field guide:

❧ Use a spreadsheet to monitor the growth of particular plants. For example, select or plant two shrubs of similar size, one in full sun, another in a shaded area. Measure their growth, record the results, enter them into a spreadsheet, turn the data into a series of graphs, and then interpret the findings. For faster results, measure the growth of quick-growing plants such as sunflowers or sweet potatoes.

❧ Select several plant species and draw a series of pictures of them as they bud, flower, and go to seed. Record information for each plant, explaining the process, and make a separate book that includes the drawings (or photos) of each stage.

❧ Exhibit the seeds that students have collected by mounting them between sheets of clear contact paper and hanging them in the window. (When you take them down, cut them into strips for journal bookmarks.) Discuss the differences between plant seeds. Can you find a seed that resembles Velcro? ❧

Bruce R. Dean is a K-12 art teacher in Uxbridge, Massachusetts, and a 1993 United States Christa McAuliffe Fellow.

Illustrations on the sample field guide page are by Roger Tory Peterson from *A Field Guide to Trees and Shrubs* by George A. Petrides (Boston: Houghton Mifflin, 1972).

Common Highbush Blueberry

(Vaccinium corymbosum)

The Highbush Blueberry is a tall shrub which can grow up to 12 feet tall. The twigs of the shrub are usually hairless and their leaves do not have ridged edges.

They are found around acid soils. Their white flowers bloom from May to June and fruits last from June up until September. The blueberry can be used for fruits, jellies, salads, pies and jams. They are found from Nova Scotia to Southern Quebec, Wisconsin to Florida to Louisiana.

Interesting fact: the fruit is the basic food for the Mourning Dove, Ruffed Grouse, Pheasant, and many songbirds.

Discovered by:
Michelle G. Student
December 1995

Sample field guide page

Learning Links for Elementary Classes

by Jeff Reading and George Taven

In the early 1990s, Olympic Heights Elementary School opened in Calgary with the typical school landscape. In a word, grass. One year later it could be summarized in two words, dead grass — at least from September through to June. An open area between two wings of the school had become a horrendous eyesore and mud bowl during the spring and fall. Rather than have the area covered with cement or gravel, several staff obtained a grant to turn it into a native plant park and natural amphitheater. We needed to enhance the schoolyard aesthetically, but we also realized that this was an opportunity to reclaim a little bit of "wilderness" for our environmental and outdoor education programs.

The links between the curriculum and the learning associated with an outdoor area became apparent even at the planning stage. Students were involved in all aspects of organizing the project, and this included calculating the quantities of soil, rock, and compost needed for the area (math); diagramming what the area would look like over time (art); writing grant requests and thank-you letters (language arts); discussing how the area might improve the quality or "wellness" of our lives (health); and researching the habitat needs of plants and the elements of ecosystems (science). While the park was being created we also invited many people into the classroom to discuss career options associated with park development, municipal planning, horticulture, technology, and community relations.

What is the area of the site? How much compost will we need? Curriculum links are apparent at every stage of a project.

Since completing our native park and amphitheater, we have found that, with a little creativity, there are literally hundreds of ways to integrate a natural area into the curriculum. When we say integrate, we do not mean "add on." Instead, we are talking about doing what we already do but doing it differently, using the outdoor classroom as a vehicle for hands-on learning. Our use of the outdoor classroom with grade five and six students has been quite extensive and continues to expand. To facilitate an integrated curriculum that fosters environmental literacy, we use a chart to plan activities in the park month by month. The intent is not to fill the chart completely, but to ensure that the park is used across the curriculum and through the seasons. The following are some of the ways that we have used our outdoor classroom.

Language Arts

❧ Have students write a play that portrays an aspect of the creation, purpose, or philosophy behind the development of the plant park from their point of view. Discuss questions such as: Why do we want a native plant park? Why are native plant parks important in a city? How is a native plant park different from a local city park? What elements are needed for a natural area such as this to survive? How do we create public interest and concern for looking after the project once it is completed?

Our students worked in groups of four to six to choose the questions they would pursue and the type of play they would script. They each wrote a rough draft and then collaborated in producing a group script. Rehearsals were held in the classroom and the amphitheater, and the plays were presented to other classes. Videotapes of the performances were sent to other schools interested in developing a native plant park, and some of the plays were presented at a "Learning Grounds" conference attended by groups interested in greening parts of their urban landscape.

◆ Have students maintain a creative journal in which they reflect on seasonal changes in the outdoor area. We sometimes ask students to make an entry without writing in the journal. This means they can ask someone else to write in it or they can make rubbings, draw pictures or diagrams, or be creative in other ways.

◆ Use the natural area for reading, either silently or aloud. We regularly stress that the plant park is a quiet place, not part of the playground where students run around and are loud.

◆ Have students write stories about how to reduce our ecological footprint, using the natural area as inspiration.

◆ Use the outdoor classroom as inspiration for poetry that is regularly added to a "poet tree" in a central location in the school.

◆ Use the plants, animals, and characteristics of the natural area as sources of new vocabulary and information for spelling programs and writing.

◆ Have students write a letter from the point of view of something in the schoolyard such as a plant, rock, or pathway.

Math

◆ During the planning process, calculate the quantities needed of materials such as rocks, topsoil, and plants, and then compare these estimated quantities to the actual amounts used.

◆ Chart sun and shade patterns over time to determine where to put various plants in order to meet their specific needs.

◆ Measure the nature area and use a grid to make a scale drawing of its layout. Record plant names and their to-scale heights and canopy size on the drawing. This can become a longitudinal study to monitor how the plants grow and change over time.

Teachers at Olympic Heights Elementary in Calgary use a chart to plan outdoor activities month by month, ensuring that the school's nature area is used across the curriculum and through the seasons.

◆ Use the outdoor classroom as a tangible place to apply math concepts such as perimeter, circumference, diameter, volume, angle, ratio and scale. For example, students can measure diameter, circumference, and ratios of plants and trees; chart and graph growth rates in plants; estimate changes in abundance and diversity of insect populations; calculate and compare the volumes of water required by various plants.

◆ Outdoor composting or indoor vermiculture are possible spinoffs of establishing a natural area in the schoolyard. Students can chart the weight of organic material that goes into the composter and compare it to the weight of what is produced.

Science

Our plant park is divided into grassland, boreal forest, and alpine ecosystems which represent those found in Alberta. Having a natural environment so close at hand enhances discussions and provides for hands-on learning about many aspects of the natural world: balanced ecosystems, food chains, communities, diversity, change, and interrelationships.

⚘ Students can explore the populations, balance within, role of, and locations of living and non-living components of an ecosystem. Using a hand lens, bug box or microscope opens up another new world to explore.

⚘ Host a community competition to design and build a bird feeder or nesting box.

⚘ Have students adopt a plant or tree, study its needs, and care for it over time.

⚘ Conduct environmental assessments that test soil, air, pollution levels, soil compacting, and so on. These studies can be extended to different environments around the community. Students may investigate questions such as how do soil conditions, the pH of soil, or the availability of water and sunlight affect plant growth and the presence of animals?

⚘ "Lasso" the earth by tossing a length of string tied into a loop. Using a kitchen knife, fork and spoon, have students explore the populations and diversities of plants, animals, and non-living items. Compare the contents of plots of equal sizes in different locations.

⚘ Explore basic scientific concepts such as erosion patterns; soil percolation and compacting; plant transpiration; the water cycle; classification of organisms and the use of identification keys; the physical make-up of soil and the impact of composting.

Social Studies

⚘ Plant native species that were used extensively by early settlers and explore the role of plants in pioneer life.

⚘ Learn the significance of plants and animals to Native peoples. If possible, involve members of local Native communities in these programs.

Health

⚘ Explore the medicinal value of plants.

⚘ Invite parents or local restaurateurs to lead cooking classes using plants or herbs grown at the school.

⚘ Use the natural area for physical education activities such as creative dance, gymnastics, tai chi, and camouflage games.

Art

⚘ Use the natural area as a place for sketching, painting, creating rubbings of natural objects, and considering the aesthetics of color schemes and patterns.

⚘ Invite a local artist to conduct a sketching or watercolor workshop in the outdoor classroom. Mount and display the finished pieces in the school.

⚘ Combine waste paper from the school with plant material to make writing paper and creative posters.

⚘ Create interpretive signs that describe the plants, their needs, their role in the ecosystem, and their use by humans. Update the signs as the natural area grows up and fills in.

Olympic Heights School

Since completing our native park and amphitheater, we have found that, with a little creativity, there are literally hundreds of ways to integrate a natural area into the curriculum.

Music

◆ Write songs about the development of the nature area, or use the area and environmental themes as inspiration for song lyrics. These songs and accompanying dance steps may be videotaped.

◆ Make "orchestra cards" that use pictures to describe natural sounds that students hear in the schoolyard.

As our native plant park and amphitheater grew, they were embraced by the entire school as well as many community members. One evening a local astronomy group held an outdoor meeting there while viewing the night sky. After school one day, six high school students were found holding a group study meeting in the amphitheater.

Now we sit back and watch it grow and develop. Creating a natural learning area on the school grounds has had nothing but a positive impact on students, staff, and community. Not only have our curriculum and learning opportunities increased, but our living and working environment has been greatly enhanced. The official opening of our native plant park and amphitheater culminated in a countdown that triggered a water sprinkler in the center of the park. As water cascaded onto the park that sunny Alberta morning, I overheard one parent say to another, "Man, we never did stuff like this when I went to school." ♪

Jeff Reading is an Environmental Education Specialist at Fish Creek Environmental Learning Centre in Calgary, Alberta. George Taven teaches at Olympic Heights Elementary School in Calgary, Alberta.

The entire school community helped to create the native plant park which is divided into grassland, boreal and alpine ecosystems.

K-12 Activities for the Outdoor Classroom

by Char Bezanson, Craig Johnson, Bill Lindquist and Nalani McCutcheon

The following activities focus on investigating local ecosystems, whether in the schoolyard or further afield. The ideas are presented in four grade level categories, but many can be adapted to several levels.

Grades K-3
Math

Landscape Tally: Take a walk to look for different colors, shapes, or objects. Have students keep a tally and make simple graphs to represent the numbers in the various categories. How would you describe your area to someone from another city or country?

Classification: Have students collect 20 or more leaves and sort them by color, shape, etc. Discuss how different classification criteria lead to different distributions. What are some of the criteria we use to classify groups of organisms such as mammals, birds, plants, and insects? How might our ordering change if we used different criteria?

Science

Wild Groceries: Discuss the position of items in a grocery store: some are on the top shelf, some are on the floor, some are stored in the basement. Have students look at the outside environment as a grocery store. What types of food are located on the top shelf (canopy), lower shelf (understory), bottom shelf (ground), and basement (underground). From what shelves do different animals "shop"? Do most animals "shop" from the same shelf, or are they evenly distributed?

Animal Tracks: Look for animal tracks in mud, sand or snow. Have students try to move their bodies in such a way as to leave track patterns similar to those they have seen. How difficult is it to move like other animals? Do you think rabbits, deer or mice would have problems walking like us? How does this relate to the concept of adaptation?

Art

Nature Crayons: Have students collect materials such as leaves, twigs, dirt, and berries, and rub them on a piece of paper to determine what color, if any, their "nature crayon" has. Have them draw a picture using these natural colors. (Caution them not to use items such as poison ivy, nettles, or live insects.)

Eyes: Have students "try on" the eyes of other animals. To simulate having an eye on the top of your head, hold a small mirror face up and level and look straight into it. Try walking a few yards with this view. For an eye on the side of the head, hold the mirror perpendicular to the ground and facing to the side. How do these views of the world differ from our own? Why do you suppose some animals have eyes in different places? What role does seeing things in different ways play in art?

Social Studies
Landscape Changes: Obtain journals of early settlers in your area and read aloud their descriptions of the landscape. Take a walk outside and make notes on how the landscape has changed since the settlers' time. How is it the same? If you, as a class, wrote a description of your landscape, what would it be? Read *Dandelions* by Eve Bunting and talk about the challenges and changes in landscape that the characters experience.

Language Arts
ABC Hike: Walk around outside looking for things that begin with the letters of the alphabet. As you come across an ant, have the students either write about or draw a picture of the ant under the letter A. See how many letters of the alphabet you can cover.

Grades 4-6
Math and Art
Signature Trees: Identify a signature tree that is representative of the trees in your area. Every year, have students measure the circumference of the trunk at chest height and determine its diameter, the diameter of the canopy, and the height of the tree. Measure the length and width of randomly selected leaves and determine average size. Compare the data from year to year. What patterns of growth do you see? Each year, take photographs of students standing next to the tree and have students draw pictures of the tree from a variety of angles. Label these carefully and save them in your schoolyard archive. Have students observe changes by comparing their photos and finished drawings with those from past years.

Science
Animal Communities: Explore animal communities that might make their home in or around the signature tree. What evidence do you see of them? What role does this tree play in the life of the woodland?

Fall Colors: As the leaves begin to change color, pull off a leaf every day and record the date. Dry the leaves in a press and laminate them on a poster with their dates. Explore pigmentation and find out the reason leaves change color.

Language Arts
Tree Tales: Have small groups of students sit silently for a short period of time next to a tree. What sounds can be heard? Where do they come from? If the tree could talk, what stories could it tell? Write a haiku, cinquain, or other poem about the tree. Read *My Side of the Mountain* by Jean Craighead George about a boy who spends a year in the woods making his home inside a carved-out hemlock tree. Write a sequel set in the school nature area.

Social Studies
Prairie Changes: Explore the role of the prairie in the lives of Native people. How did it change as the Europeans moved in? How did their attitude toward the prairies differ? Let students sit quietly in the prairie and imagine what life was like. What is the future of prairies in North America? (This can be adapted for other ecosystems.)

Greening School Grounds

Grades 7-8

Art

Nature in Art: Look at illustrations and paintings of landscapes and natural objects such as leaves, shells, twigs, and stones. What is the artist trying to communicate — a feeling, an impression, a detail, or technical information? What are some different ways that artists might represent the same object? Have students pick an item or a feature (a tree, a twig, dry grass) and represent it in different ways, perhaps focusing on line, color or "impression" one day, and on accurate proportions and specific details on another. What are the advantages of each?

Social Studies

Medicinal Herbs: Research plants that were used by Native people and early European settlers as medicinal herbs. Collaborate with a local naturalist to determine if any of these plants grows locally. Are they native or were they brought to North America by European settlers? Are any still in use? (Examples: coneflower, golden seal, ginseng, chamomile, peppermint.) Conduct a field trip to point out local medicinal herbs and try some herbal teas made from them. Plan a garden of native medicinal herbs for your school ground. Useful references: Kelly Kindscher *Medicinal Wild Plants of the Prairie* (University of Kansas Press, 1992); Laura C. Martin, *Wildflower Folklore* (Globe Pequot Press, 1984).

Science

Seed Strategies: In autumn, collect dry seed heads from wildflowers and have students draw, dissect, and analyze them with the following questions in mind: In which part of the seed head are the seeds? Do some appear to be more ripe than others? What strategy does the plant use to distribute its seed? Are all the seeds released at once, or a few at a time? Does seed distribution depend on animals, wind, or something else? How do the characteristics of the seed increase its chances of finding a good place to grow? How are dry seeds different from seeds in fleshy fruits? What is the function of the fleshy fruit?

Sowing Wild Seeds: Try germinating wildflower seeds by rolling them in a moist paper towel and putting the towel in a plastic bag. Keep the bag in a warm place for a week or two. How are wild seeds different from seeds we buy? Do germination rates differ between species? Have students research seed dormancy. What purpose does dormancy serve?

Language Arts

No Uncertain Terms: Investigate the need for specialized terminology. In autumn, collect several different kinds of grasses, including seed heads. Have students describe the grasses in detail without using any specialized terms. Post all the descriptions of each species together. How much alike are they? How long are they? Could you be sure which grass was being described?

Teach a short lesson on grass terminology, including terms such as blade, sheath, node, inflorescence, and spikelet. Have students describe the grasses again, using the new terms they have learned. Compare the descriptions. How similar are the descriptions now? How long are they? What conclusions can we draw about specialized terms? When is it beneficial to use them, and when does using them interfere with communication? (This activity could also be done with dry seed heads.) Reference: Lauren Brown, *Grasses: An Identification Guide* (Houghton-Mifflin, 1979).

Grades 9-12

Language Arts

Life Like a River: Discuss the concept of watersheds and the idea that rivers and lakes develop characteristics which reflect the journeys of the water flowing into them. Extend this to consider the concept of cultural watersheds. How did people flow to this place? What experiences did they have in getting here? How does the community reflect the characteristics of the people living there? Visit a river or stream and compare in writing the role and growth of the river with your own. Begin with questions such as: How old is the river? What are the signs of its age? How is it viewed? Who depends upon it? Compare/contrast what you have observed about the river with your own growth and responsibilities. At this point in your life, how are you viewed? What are your responsibilities? Who depends on you?

Science

Foot Loading: The ability to travel through snow to obtain food and shelter is crucial to many animals. It is influenced by the physical characteristics of both the snow and the animals' feet and legs. Heavier animals generally have larger feet and longer legs than lighter animals. One way to study how different animals move through snow is to compare foot loads, or an animal's mass per unit foot area. To compare foot loads, the following foot load index is used: 100 minus (body mass in grams/foot area in cm²)/10.

Have students calculate their body mass in kilograms and their foot area in centimeters. Then go outside and measure foot penetration in undisturbed and packed snow. Construct a graph showing the relationship between foot load indexes and foot penetration. Calculate the foot load index of a pet cat or dog and compare. Look for and identify tracks in snow and discuss the implications of foot size for animals living in snowy environments.

Math

Weighty Water: Measure how much water comes down when it rains. First, calculate the area of the schoolyard. Measure the next rainfall and calculate the volume of water that fell on the school grounds (depth x area). Compare this volume to quantities the students would recognize. For added effect have the students calculate the weight of this water (1 cubic foot weighs 28.4 kg or 62.5 lbs; 1 cubic meter weighs 1000 kg or 2205 lbs.). Discuss where all this water goes.

Personal and Family Life

Animal Clans: Throughout history cultures have used clan animals to create or express a closeness to the natural world. Ask students to list the living things that inhabit your nature area (whether observed or not) and discuss the characteristics of a few of the species. Tell the students they will be forming "clans" and selecting a plant or animal that best represents their traits. Each group should research several species, select one that is representative of their group, and list qualities of their clan species that they find inspiring and want to foster in their own lives. Create visual displays that highlight these traits and introduce the clan to the rest of the class. ◈

Activities developed by members of the School Nature Area Project in Northfield, Minnesota: Nalani McCutcheon (K-3), Bill Lindquist (4-6), Char Bezanson (7-8), and Craig Johnson (9-12).

K-12 Learning in a Schoolyard Prairie

 prairie restoration project provides opportunities to study ecological concepts and the natural and cultural history of a site. Most of these ideas can be adapted for use in any outdoor classroom and in any grade level.

Grades K-5

Science

Make crayon rubbings of prairie grasses. ❧ Visualize and describe life as a prairie ant. ❧ Observe butterfly pollination and nectar-collecting behavior. ❧ Observe a monarch chrysalis and butterfly. ❧ Dissect and examine prairie soil. ❧ Compare biodiversity in a prairie and a lawn. ❧ Collect seed from a prairie restoration or remnant. ❧ Make and use dyes from prairie plants. ❧ Have a scavenger hunt for plant adaptations. ❧ Hypothesize and test leaf orientation frequency in the compass plant. ❧ Measure and compare air pollution at potential restoration sites. ❧ Adopt a species to research, grow, and transplant into the restoration site.

by Robin Greenler

Language Arts

Read and listen to accounts from early settlers. ❧ Learn the first sounds and letters of the names of prairie plants through a movement game. ❧ Record monthly observations from a single prairie spot. ❧ Create a fictional journal of an early prairie settler or Native person. ❧ Write a poem or haiku for a plant. ❧ Write a dialogue between a plant and a pollinator. ❧ Take a single-sense walk in the prairie. ❧ Develop materials describing the restoration project to the public.

Math

Identify geometric shapes in prairie plants. ❧ Determine the migratory route of monarch butterflies and calculate the distance they fly. ❧ Grow a prairie plant and observe, measure and graph the root, shoot, and leaf growth. ❧ Determine height of trees and buildings on the restoration site. ❧ Solve word problems concerning number of seeds, amount of seed, cost of seed.

Social Studies

Find local town and landmark names which reflect a prairie heritage. ❧ Design a prairie celebration. ❧ Study the introduction of non-native plants to North America.

Art and Music

Create a plant identification booklet with solar graphics. ❧ Model life cycle stages of the monarch. ❧ Listen to "Flight of the Bumblebee" and create your own insect symphony. ❧ Design and model a hypothetical "best" seed. ❧ Create signs describing the project to the public. ❧ Discover which musical instruments best mimic bird calls.

Grades 6-12

Science

Examine and calculate the grass-to-forb ratio in a prairie. ✦ Calculate the percentage of "edge" in a prairie remnant. ✦ Compare prairie-based diets to your own. ✦ Observe and record phenological sequences of color, blossoming and insect life. ✦ Examine single prairie niches and then fit them together. ✦ Measure biodiversity in a prairie and lawn. ✦ Adopt a species to research, grow, transplant, tag, and follow in restoration. ✦ Experiment with methods of site preparation and weed control.

M.E. Gartshore

Language Arts

Read the works of prairie authors and poets. ✦ Create a fictional journal of an early prairie settler or Native. ✦ Write a sonnet or haiku for a plant. ✦ Interview area residents about local history. ✦ Write a letter to a great grandparent or grandchild explaining your restoration efforts. ✦ Write about a seed's journey to North America from its native home. ✦ Develop signs and pamphlets describing the restoration project to the public. ✦ Write, lay out, and distribute a prairie newsletter.

Math

Develop a plant purchase plan based on project budget and desired seed list. ✦ Calculate total prairie acreage consumed by large cities. ✦ Graph seed weight and total seed set. ✦ Graph phenological sequences. ✦ Estimate biomass of the prairie and compare to other ecosystems. ✦ Map the proposed restoration site. ✦ Compare various seeding-rate recommendations. ✦ Correlate insect gall presence with plant height and size.

Social Studies

Research local settlement and prairie land use. ✦ Research the origin of local town and landmark names which reflect a prairie heritage. ✦ Research land ownership records of the school and restoration site.

Nalani McCutcheon

Art and Music

Develop a pictorial key to prairie species. ✦ Create a video or slide show to document the restoration project. ✦ Produce a photo essay of a plant's life cycle. ✦ Compose and perform songs based on accounts from early settlers. ✦ Create a prairie soundscape. ✦ Create posters to display results of experiments.

Students can research prairie land use and write a dialogue between a plant and a pollinator.

Robin Greenler teaches biology at Beloit College in Beloit, Wisconsin.

*The schoolyard
nature area as
an inspiration
for the arts*

by Karen Krupa

The Abundance of Nature's Imagination

As an artist, I am often struck by people's heightened creativity when they are exposed to the sensual fecundity of nature. When our Home and School association decided to transform an asphalt playground into an environmental learning center, I saw the potential for the schoolyard to be integrated into the arts curriculum. I could not resist the opportunity to foster the children's creative responses by surrounding them with the cyclical beauty of nature.

It has always saddened me to see how elitist art becomes as children progress from the non-judgmental joyfulness of mark-making in kindergarten to the self-conscious "I'm not an artist" withdrawal in the upper grades. This narrowing definition of what is and is not art creates students who do not believe in the validity of their unique visions and are reluctant to express themselves. Nature offers another model of creativity — one of infinite diversity and equality. I believe that by pointing out the endless variety of natural forms and by immersing students in the sensual pleasures of texture, aroma, and color, teachers can help older children to rediscover their own artistic voices and to express them with abandon. Following are some of the art activities that have been inspired by plantings in our schoolyard.

Karen Krupa

*Weaving a giant basket to protect
a young tree.*

Natural Dyes

A quick glance at a landscape or a handful of leaves will prove the expression "forty shades of green" to be a gross understatement. Yet so often students are limited to the colors of paints straight from the bottle and color mixing is discouraged because it is considered messy or wasteful. Many children cannot imagine unusual color or begin to understand how to achieve it. A magical way to help children broaden their color palette is by extracting colors from plants to create natural dyes.

Many readily available plant stuffs will create color on cloth. In the fall, gather goldenrod (fresh flowering tops or roots) or apple bark (ask for prunings when you go apple picking). In the winter, ask your grocer for onion skins or collect pine cones. In the spring, try forsythia (fresh flowering tops) or bracken fern. Natural dyes are always a surprise because it is hard to predict exactly what color you will achieve. Natural colors are complex and luminous, and the color of the dyed cloth is not necessarily the color of the plant. Wool cloth dyes best, but cotton, linen, and silk can also be used. You can dye fleece and felt it; yarn, and knit or weave it; or fabric, and quilt or embroider with it.

Natural dyeing is simple. You will need good ventilation, a stove or hot plate, large pots and buckets, stirring spoons, strainer, washed cloth or yarn, plant material, and alum (available at pharmacies and grocery stores). Gather enough plant material to equal the weight of your cloth. Cover the plants with water and let them soak overnight. Simmer them for one hour and then strain the liquid into a bucket. (Compost the solid plant waste.) Return the dye to a pot on the hot plate. For each pound of cloth add four tablespoons of alum, which opens the fibers and allows the dye to penetrate and become colorfast. Wet the cloth and then sink it into dye bath. Simmer for one hour, stirring frequently. Cloth can be removed from the dye bath after an hour or left to soak overnight. Rinse well. The cloth can be folded or twisted and tied to create tie-dye patterns, or overdyed in a different plant dye bath to create richer, more complex colors.

Papermaking

Papermaking is another simple way to transform plant fibers through artistic alchemy. Choose the leaves of long-fiber plants such as day lily, iris, corn, gladiolus, or bullrush. Chop, soak, boil, and blend the leaves to create a pulp. Then cast the pulp into sheets of paper which can be used for bookmaking, collaging, painting, drawing, and writing. (Detailed papermaking procedures can be found in many arts and crafts books; see reference list on next page.)

Leaf Printing

Leaf printing is a simple technique with vast possibilities for classroom extensions. Apply tempera paint to any leaf, place the leaf on paper with the paint side down, cover the leaf with newspaper, and press on it by rolling or rubbing over the newspaper. Children are delighted by these instant, easily repeated prints. They can make designs with the prints, create cards, or study the nutrient highways represented by the leaf-vein patterns. They can make a map of all the plants in their garden and use the leaf prints as aids in identification. They can ask pen pals to send exotic leaves, print them on a map, and study habitat diversity.

The Goddess of Garrison Creek

Tree Baskets

Sometimes the recreational use of a playground can conflict with a naturalization effort. In our schoolyard a newly planted orchard was endangered because the soil around the young tree roots was being compacted. To give the trees and roots time to grow strong enough to withstand the traffic, a local basket weaver was hired to work with classes to weave giant protective baskets (three feet high and four feet in diameter) around each apple tree. The children designed the shape of each basket fence, prepared the materials, and took turns twining cedar bark, dogwood, grapevine, and brambles around willow uprights. While designed on a monumental scale, the baskets were made of a temporal material that will eventually decompose and provide nutrients for the trees once the protection is no longer needed. An unanticipated extension of the project was that some of the willow uprights sent out roots to a creek that had been buried under the schoolyard for nearly a century. The living baskets sprouted new leaves! Although the students had studied the history of their schoolyard and knew of the existence of the underground stream, they were amazed by this manifestation of nature's regenerative powers.

The infinite variety of the natural world helps young artists to treasure their own unique styles and to feel connected to the evocative magic of living, growing things.

Artistic experiences which tap into the cyclical vein of nature are vitally important for youth, especially those who are surrounded by urban ugliness and decay. The infinite variety of the natural world helps young artists to treasure their own unique styles and to feel connected to the evocative magic of living, growing things. Our schoolyard garden has proved art to be a powerful tool in increasing students' self-esteem and belief in their artistic expressions, in building a sense of community, and in fostering creative responses to problems. ﻬ

Karen Krupa is an artist and parent who worked on a schoolyard greening project at Ossington Old Orchard School in Toronto, Ontario.

References

The following books explain the techniques of these artistic activities in greater detail.

General Inspiration
Rubinov, Jacobson. *Drinking Lightning: Art, Creativity and Transformation*. Boston: Shambala, 2000. ISBN 1-57062-746-0.

Leafprinting
Sohi, Morteza E. *Look What I Did With a Leaf!* New York: Walker and Company, 1993. ISBN 0-80277-440-7.

Natural Dyes
Sandberg, Gosta. *The Red Dyes*. Ashville, North Carolina: Lark Books, 1994. ISBN 1-88737-417-5.

Wells, Kate. *Fabric Dyeing and Printing*. Loveland, Colorado: Interweave Press, 1997. ISBN 1-88301-035-7.

Van Stralen, Trudy. *Indigo, Madder and Marigold*. Loveland, Colorado: Interweave Press, 1993. ISBN 0-93402-686-6.

Felting
Brown, Victoria. *Feltwork*. New York: Lorenz Books, 1996. ISBN 1-85967-297-3.

Papermaking
Elliot, M., Jones, J., Mansfield, J., and Stone, S. *The Art and Craft of Paper*. London: Premier Editions, 1995. ISBN 1-89773-016-0.

Hiebert, Helen, *Papermaking With Plants*. Pownal, Vermont: Storey Books, 1998. ISBN 1-58017-087-0.

Plowman, John. *The Craft of Handmade Paper*. New York: Knickerbocker, 1997. ISBN 1-57715-018-X.

Shadow Puppets
Cleaver, Elizabeth. *The Enchanted Caribou*. Toronto: Oxford University Press, 1985.

Basketweaving
Harvey, Virginia I. *The Techniques of Basketry*. Seattle: University of Washington Press, 1986.

Math in the Schoolyard

 schoolyard is a convenient setting for many math activities and is especially suited to concept application and problem-solving. Number sense, patterns and relationships, measurement, estimation, geometry, statistics and probability — mathematics is, at its root, a way of describing the world and its patterns. A nature area and the objects and phenomena within it can be estimated, counted, and measured, and the data collected can then be charted, tabled, averaged, graphed, and manipulated in many ways. We might teach fractions or percentages using pizzas or dollars, but these concepts can be extended by having students come up with ways to estimate the fraction of the sky covered by clouds or determine the percentage of their schoolyard that consists of asphalt or of lawn.

by Char Bezanson and Judy Killion

One of the best things about using the schoolyard for teaching is that it provides a direct connection to "the real world." And the real world isn't neatly divided into subject areas. Any activity done in a natural setting provides an opportunity for students and teachers to "double-dip," meeting learning objectives in more than one area. A first-grade activity that involves measuring, counting, or sorting leaves may have as its primary objective the development of number sense and other math skills, but it also provides opportunities to observe texture, color, insect interactions, and the unity and diversity of life. Fifth-graders looking for patterns in the angles formed by twigs are fulfilling a geometry objective while simultaneously gaining experience with plant structure that can be built on in a science lesson, or which might inspire a poem or a painting.

In middle and secondary grades, concrete applications of math concepts in a schoolyard setting are especially useful in developing skills in divergent thinking. Middle-schoolers can devise a variety of ways to estimate quantities such as the surface area of a pond, the height of a tree, or the mass of a tree trunk, and determine the "best" solution for the specific problem to be solved. (For example, which method would be best for calculating the biomass, firewood, or board-feet contained in a tree? Which would be most precise? Which would involve the simplest tools?) Applying math skills in these ways helps students develop confidence in their ability to solve problems in other contexts and to design their own scientific investigations. High school students can learn about statistical sampling by documenting the number of species along a transect or in a series of study plots, and thus understand how they might apply such mathematical tools to learning about ecosystem diversity or other related topics.

Young girls explore patterns and diversity through counting and measuring; an older student applies statistical sampling in an ecosystem study.

Standards documents, state and provincial curriculum frameworks, textbooks, and other curriculum materials often include lessons and illustrations drawn from the real world. Many of these can be adapted to the schoolyard. Since no two schoolyards are the same, this adaptation does require forethought and creativity on the part of teachers. But the increase in student interest, motivation, and learning easily makes this investment of time worthwhile. Some starters are presented here, but once you begin using your outdoor classroom for math you're sure to come up with many more ideas.

Prairies Have a Lot of Gall

ROUND GALLS THAT MAKE A PLANT LOOK AS IF IT HAS SWALLOWED A ping-pong ball are common on the stems of Canada goldenrod (*Solidago canadensis*). The gall is a growth formed by the plant in response to the larva of the goldenrod gall fly, *Eurosta solidaginis*. In summer, the female fly lays an egg in the unfolded leaves of the plant's top-most bud. After hatching, the larva tunnels into the growing tip and causes the plant to grow a ball-like deformation, forming a protective home for the hungry, growing larva. If it is lucky, the larva  spends the entire winter in this chamber, emerging from the gall in early spring. Often, however, galls are pecked open in winter by chickadees or other hungry birds.

Sampling Activity: Since galls are large, obvious, and stationary, they are easy to observe and count, allowing students to practice sampling techniques while learning about plant-insect interactions. In the following activity, students count goldenrod galls in a small area in order to estimate the number of galls in a large area. If Canada goldenrod is not plentiful in your area, a local botanist or entomologist should be able to suggest an alternative (thousands of insects induce galls on a wide range of host plants).

1. Identify and examine goldenrod plants with ball galls. Cut one open to demonstrate the presence of the insect larva.

2. Measure the study area by using a tape or by pacing it off. Estimate the total area, mapping it if desired.

3. Choose several sample plots to count. For example, if your site has an area of 800 square meters, and you have 10 pairs of students, you could have each pair count the goldenrod galls in a plot measuring four square meters. Have students consider: What are some different ways to distribute the sample squares across the site? Which might be best, and why? (For example, you might try to avoid bias by choosing sample squares randomly, or in some regular pattern across the site.)

4. Assign a pair of students to each plot. When they have tallied their results, have each pair use only their own data to predict the number of galls on the whole site. Now, using data from all of the plots, determine the average number of galls per four-square-meter sample and estimate the number on the site. Is this number the same as the prediction? Which estimate do you think is more accurate?

Extension: Students can count the number of goldenrod stems and the number of galls to determine the average number of galls per plant. Could this number be less than one? Both the number of goldenrod stems and the number and percentage of galls can be monitored from year to year in an area. — *Char Bezanson*

Primary Grade Activities

Patterns

Have students sort a collection of items (leaves, shells, rocks), using their own criteria (color, shape, size), and have other students try to "guess the rule." Have children look for patterns in the schoolyard: the way leaves position themselves on stems, the number and arrangement of petals on the flower, the way the plants are planted in the garden areas, the way the fence is made.

Number sense

Count and graph plants or animals in the schoolyard. For example, on the first visit to a spring bulb garden students may count five purple crocuses and ten yellow ones. They then use squares of colored paper to make a histogram, one square per flower. As flowers come into bloom, the graph grows. While in the schoolyard, watch for the teachable moment. Example: There are birds on the fence, on the telephone lines, on the lawn. Count them, and then watch for one of them to fly away or another to arrive. Have students make a math sentence that tells what happened (7 sparrows – 2 sparrows = 5 sparrows) and illustrate the story problem on their clipboards.

Geometry

Go on a shape hunt to locate geometric shapes in the playground, gardens, and walkways. Give students a tally sheet with the shapes they are to look for and have them tally each time they find that shape. Extension: Have students draw the shapes and graph how many of each shape they found.

Measurement

Have students look for things to measure in the schoolyard, using both standard units and non-standard units. How many hand-widths wide is the path? How many steps? How would you measure an ant? What do you do when the plant is higher than the ruler? Practice using measuring tools: measure rainfall using rain gauges, temperature using thermometers, distance using tape measures, rulers, or string.

Graphing

Measure, count, and graph things that change over time such as temperatures, rainfall, the height of plants, the number of flowers in bloom, the length of shadows.

Intermediate and Middle School Activities

Collecting and describing data

After listing some characteristics of their schoolyard, have students choose a subject on which to collect and graph data, such as heights, numbers, or circumferences of trees; lengths of stems between leaves; number of anthills per square meter. Collect and graph weather data over time. Create graphs to show how the temperature and rainfall in your area compare with those in another area of the country or world, using the Internet or the newspaper for reference.

Number operations

Have students observe the outdoor classroom and record activities taking place in the form of word problems and mathematical sentences. Challenge them to find as many addition, subtraction, multiplication, and division stories as they can. Create a Playground Math Book with illustrations of these story problems and the math sentences that go with them. For example: The entire fourth grade is out playing softball. If there are two fourth-grade classes of 27 students each, and three softball fields, how many students are on each softball team if the students are evenly distributed in the fields?

Skid Crease

Geometry

Have students use measured lengths of rope to create various geometric shapes and then calculate their perimeter and area. Find ways to estimate the area of irregular shapes. Identify and measure geometric shapes on the playground such as gardens and walkways, calculate their areas, and come up with related questions: How much fencing would be needed to fence a certain area of the playground? There are 450 students in our school. If they were all on the playground at one time how much space would each child have if we divided the area equally?

Measurement and estimation

Have a contest in which students measure and record everything they can find that is measurable within an allotted period of time. If they find something they think cannot be measured, such as a tall tree, have them make a note of it so the class can brainstorm whether it is indeed something that cannot be measured. If it cannot be measured precisely, can it be estimated? What strategies could be used? ❧

Char Bezanson is an ecologist and Regional Educator for the School Nature Area Project and teaches in the Education Department at St. Olaf College in Northfield, Minnesota. Judy Killion teaches fifth grade math and science at Christie Elementary in Plano, Texas.

Any activity done in a natural setting provides an opportunity for students and teachers to "double-dip," meeting learning objectives in more than one area.

Exploring Food and Culture through Gardening

by Nicole Thibault

here I live, in the culturally diverse neighborhood of Strathcona near downtown Vancouver, I often go for weekend walks down the alleys, peering into backyard gardens for ideas. I recognize Chinese gardens by the use of unique supports such as twigs and branches, and the non-linear, intensive method of planting. Italian gardens often have a multi-dimensional appearance: zucchini wind their tendrils up trellises and beans climb cornstalks for support; shade-givers and shade-lovers are interplanted. The methods and fruits of the gardeners' labors reflect a diversity of culture and geography, but there is evidence, too, of convergent adaptation to this shared urban habitat: every square inch of garden space is used. Vegetable plots are not relegated to backyards, but are also incorporated in front yards among rose bushes, fig trees and marigolds. It is not unusual to see a front yard full of overwintering onions, or Chinese cabbages lining the walk.

A big part of culture is food. But what we eat and the way in which food is grown, prepared and celebrated varies greatly from culture to culture. Using food and gardening as the basis for exploring culture and geography provides many possibilities for classroom inquiry and school gardening projects. It can also be a bridge to your community. In school communities that have large numbers of immigrant students, for instance, a multicultural school vegetable garden can open doors to the meaningful involvement of parents whose participation in school activities might otherwise be limited by language barriers.

The following ideas will get you started:

❧ Research how people of different cultures design their gardens. The class might go on a city-wide tour that takes in a diverse array of gardens from richer to poorer neighborhoods. A local gardening club may be able to help put you in touch with gardeners who would be willing to show off their gardens and answer questions about what they grow and how they grow it. Have students bring along clipboards to sketch and take notes. Back in the classroom, discuss the similarities and differences in the structure and patterns of various gardens.

⤳ Invite parents or other gardeners from various ethnic groups in your community to speak to the class about their gardening methods. This will provide an opportunity for students to learn more about why people garden as they do, thus appreciating the context behind the different gardening strategies. Focus on how the particular history of each cultural group and the geography of their native lands has shaped their gardens.

⤳ Drawing on the expertise (and seed supplies!) of gardeners from local ethnic communities, incorporate some of their native foods and garden designs in the school's garden plot. Students might choose to group vegetables of similar types (root vegetables here, salad greens there) or to divide the plot along ethnic or geographical lines (Chinese vegetables in one area, African vegetables in another).

⤳ Invite elders from local First Nations to share their knowledge of plants indigenous to your area. This will open the door to ethnobotany, an important new field of scientific inquiry. Elders can explain the healing properties and spiritual significance of local flora. Apart from improving intercultural understanding, this exploration provides an important opportunity for students to appreciate the ecological importance of many native plants.

⤳ Research the many festivals and celebrations centering on the planting and harvesting of food around the world. Many of these celebrate the changing of the seasons and give thanks for the gifts received from the earth. It is a way to teach children that most of what they need to survive comes from the dark rich tilth that gives life to plants.

No matter where we live in the world, and regardless of skin color or language, we all have a basic need for plants to provide sustenance, clean air and shelter. Schoolyard gardening offers students a hands-on opportunity to expand their awareness and deepen their understanding of how the peoples of the world go about meeting these basic needs. ❧

Nicole Thibault teaches grades one and two at Jessie Wowk Elementary School in Richmond, British Columbia.

A multicultural school vegetable garden can open doors to the meaningful involvement of parents whose participation in school activities might otherwise be limited by language barriers.

Teaching in a classroom without walls can be discomforting at first. Keeping a few pointers in mind will enhance the learning and enjoyment for everyone.

Tips and Tricks for Taking Kids Outside

In the middle of the night, are you jolted from your bed by nightmarish images of children running hither and yon in the wilderness as you take them out to investigate water quality in the nearby stream, play a predator-prey game, or study the life cycle of monarchs? If so, you are not alone. However, many educators have tackled these fears and made such adventures seem routine. It just takes practice, and keeping in mind a few key guidelines.

by Nalani McCutcheon and Andrea Swanson

Have clear expectations

Before you walk out the door and into the wilderness — or even into the schoolyard — with your very excited and enthusiastic class, discuss behavioral expectations. This conversation can make or break your time together outside. Allowing students to help determine expectations (including the agreement to have expectations in the first place) sets up an atmosphere of mutual respect and ensures greater understanding of the rules and a greater willingness to follow them. Make a list of a few specific behaviors and state them in the positive. For example, an expectation that there will be "no yelling and screaming" may have the same intent as "use quiet voices," but the latter is a positive statement of the specific behavior you wish to see.

By putting the wind at her back and the sun in her eyes, a teacher makes sure everyone can see and hear.

Plan the logistics

❧ Have a clear signal for getting everyone's attention and gathering together. It helps to practice it before you go outside.

❧ Discuss where you will gather when you get outside. If you will be on trails, establish clear meeting places such as trail intersections and trail heads.

❧ Explain to students that if they get separated from the group, they should sit down and wait. Someone will come and look for them.

❧ Decide who will lead the group as you travel down the trail. Create opportunities for children to take turns leading.

❧ Provide opportunities to walk and run. Let children know that this will happen.

❧ Use a variety of group sizes. Have students spend some time working in large groups, small groups, pairs and independently.

❧ To help focus attention, give specific assignments.

❧ Know your agenda and plans and let your students know what you are thinking while still being open to teachable moments.

❧ Discuss safety. If you will be near water, clearly explain the potential hazards. If you will be walking in the hot sun, make sure there is drinking water for everyone, sunscreen on exposed skin, and hats on heads. If you are using snowshoes or cross-country skis, discuss their appropriate use. Bring a first aid kit and, if someone is allergic to bees, a bee sting kit.

⁕ Be ready for any kind of weather and dress appropriately. Bring extra mittens, hats, and boots if necessary. Rain gear and warm coats will make an enormous difference in the outcome of your outdoor activity.

⁕ Evaluate your time together when you return indoors. Discuss what went well and what didn't. Gather suggestions for activities and behavioral expectations for future trips outside.

Practice and model activities

Having clear assignments for students to complete when they go outdoors will help focus their attention. And whether it is a paper-and-pencil activity or an active game that illustrates an ecological concept, your expectations will be clearer to students if you practice before going outside. Even as you head out the door, you may want to have a few practice runs at gathering together using your signal. That way, you too can enjoy the experience outside and not have to worry continually about gathering the flock. The clearer your goals and expectations, the safer and more comfortable children will feel. This added comfort will increase their willingness to participate and complete their work.

Dave Donkers

Whenever possible, model what you want your students to do by becoming an active participant yourself. For example, if your students are drawing or writing in their journals along the trail, you should do it as well. This not only demonstrates that you value the activity; it is also an opportunity to show your students that you too are a student.

Be flexible

No matter how wonderful a teacher you are, natural lessons outdoors will sometimes be more compelling than the task at hand. The turkey vulture soaring overhead or the rabbit running across the trail may interrupt your lesson, but accept that it is a natural attention magnet for students. Take the broader view of learning and turn these opportunities to your advantage. They are the moments your students will likely never forget, and if you can bridge these spontaneous events to the lesson at hand, you will likely cement the learning. Your challenge is to find the bridge — and there will be one. The great thing about the natural world is that everything is connected to everything else.

Nalani McCutcheon

Focus attention with specific assignments, and plan for both group and independent activities.

Communicate strategically

In communicating with students outdoors, be prepared to face noise, atmospheric conditions, and other distractions that you cannot control. Take a lesson from the interpretive field and keep the following in mind:

⁕ Make sure the sun is in your eyes; then you can be sure that it isn't in your students' eyes.

⁕ Put the wind to your back. This will push the sound of your voice toward the students.

⁕ As you talk to students, try to reduce the distance between your mouth and their ears. Unless you are working with older students, this means kneeling down when talking. This keeps your voice from being lost in the wind, and it gives you a better perspective on what the world looks like from their view.

Structure your lessons to take advantage of the opportunities available while remembering the potential challenges. A trip to the pond is full of exciting learning possibilities, but there are wet shoes and clothing to think about as well.

↣ If you are on a narrow trail and some students are having trouble seeing or hearing, have students form a double-file line. Stop the group, step off the trail, and walk toward the middle of the group. Have the students turn to face the side of the trail you are on, and have those in the front row kneel down. That way, everyone can see and hear without tromping off the trail.

↣ If you see something that you want to look at as a group (and it is appropriate to walk off the trail to it), lead the students in a single or double-file line behind you, and form a circle around it. You step into the center, and everyone can see.

↣ If you are on a trail you use often, place flags or markers along the way. Then if you want to allow students to travel up ahead of you, you can tell them to move at their own pace, but to stop at the next flag.

Carry props

When you first get started, you may fear that moment of having unfocused students and not knowing how to redirect their attention. Many teachers use a prop bag in which are packed focusing games (nature bingo, scavenger hunts, recipe of a forest), natural artifacts (seeds, leaves, antlers, fur samples, feathers), hand lenses, binoculars, and other aids. When you need to focus students' attention, pull an appropriate item out of the bag. Students usually can't wait to see what will come out next. In fact, you may find that you want to continue to use this even after you gain proficiency in taking your students outside.

Empower yourself

Let's face it, to be a good teacher, you have to know yourself. You must have clear expectations and personal goals, and a sense of their priority so you can monitor and adjust in a heartbeat to assure that the end result is satisfactory. If indeed the best learning lies on the edge of chaos, then in order to be comfortable there, you need to be sure of your footing when you are close to that line. Just as an athlete takes time to practice on a new field before a competition, so too must teachers take time to establish a personal comfort with the new learning environment.

Prior to taking your students outside, visit the area and become familiar with it. Visualize in your mind where your students will be during different parts of the lesson and what areas you want to make sure they avoid. Structure your lessons to take advantage of the opportunities available while remembering the potential challenges. A trip to the pond is full of exciting learning possibilities, but there are wet shoes and clothing to think about as well.

The size of your group should depend on your comfort level. Some people enjoy larger groups of 20 to 25 while others prefer groups of 10 to 15. Bringing additional adults to assist with your outdoor adventure can be helpful, and most schools have policies that require a certain ratio of children to adults. It helps to make sure the supporting adults are aware of your expectations, both of the children and of them.

Finally, remember that your level of comfort is not built by your classroom walls; it is built within your mind. If you set clear expectations, plan ahead, and follow a few key guidelines, you will eliminate most potential stumbling blocks. You will also find that your outdoor excursions will be more fun for everyone, including you. Now sleep well! ↯

Nalani McCutcheon is Executive Director and Andrea Swanson is Regional Educator at the School Nature Area Project at St. Olaf College in Northfield, Minnesota.

Service Learning: Connecting Classrooms with Communities

nvironmental educators have long known the value of linking learning to issues in the "real world": learning is not only enhanced when it has links to the community, but it is more engaging and rewarding. Moreover, by tackling problems and serving real needs within the community, students begin to see that their own decisions and actions can help to improve the quality of life for all. This integration of learning with public service and outreach is at the heart of service learning, a pedagogy which has students identify problems or needs in their communities, use critical thinking skills to propose solutions, and take action to effect change. Now mandated in many school districts, service learning can involve students in a wide variety of public service projects and frequently its focus is on improving the health and diversity of local environments.

by Mary Haque

Gary Pennington

A "greening" project, whether it occurs on the school grounds, in a local park, or in community gardens, opens up many excellent opportunities for students to engage in service learning. For example, elementary school children might use part of their schoolyard garden to grow vegetables for a local food bank. Middle school students might share the knowledge and skills gained in their own schoolyard project by installing a garden or nature area at a retirement home, a hospital, or a shelter for abused children. Students at all grade levels might reduce their school's greenhouse gas emissions and save taxpayers' dollars by planting trees that help to cool the building in the heat of summer and insulate it from the prevailing winds of winter. High school students could estimate the impact of such a project over the long term and write an article for a local newspaper informing the public of the benefits of landscaping for energy efficiency.

In schools where students have created habitats for wildlife or installed trails through wooded areas, they might also undertake a number of projects that will enhance the public use and enjoyment of the nature area. For example, students might make interpretive signs and identifying labels for trees and shrubs; or they might design and distribute a pamphlet to the local community describing native plants on the school grounds and inviting people to use the area outside of school hours. Older students might write and illustrate a book for elementary school students about the value of native plants to wildlife and help the younger students plan and plant their own nature trail.

Elementary school children might use part of their schoolyard garden to grow vegetables for a local food bank.

Teachers whose school grounds projects are still in the planning stage might devise simpler service learning projects. For example, "Flower Power" is a service learning project at Morrison Elementary School in which each student grows a flower from seed in a cup as part of a science class. On one special day each year, the elderly clients of the local Meals on Wheels program receive, along with their hand-delivered hot meal, a fresh flower with a note from the child who grew it.

In many cases, service learning begins in partnerships between schools and non-profit organizations or universities. For example, in South Carolina, students and faculty at Clemson University partnered with at-risk elementary students enrolled in an after-school program sponsored by the South Carolina Botanical Garden. Together they helped Habitat for Humanity homeowners landscape their new yards, installing trees, shrubs, bulbs, ground covers, vegetables, herbs, bird houses, and butterfly gardens. The director of the after-school program observed that the children "sprouted wings" when they discovered where their food comes from, created nature crafts, and learned about horticulture through their community service project.

Clemson University student helps children make pine cone bird feeders as part of a service learning project.

Outcomes or "deliverables" are often an important part of service learning. In a project called Clemson Looks at Sustainable Schools, Clemson University students worked with four schools to develop landscape plans emphasizing water conservation, energy efficiency, wildlife habitat, and low maintenance. They also prepared a presentation on environmental stewardship and landscape maintenance to share with schools, volunteers, and the public. Student-created posters about the project were used at Earth Day celebrations, service-learning meetings and open houses; and curricula reflecting state science standards were developed using the landscape plan. K-12 students increased public awareness of the project by hosting a Sustainability Fair.

Service learning projects can promote individual learning and provide a process through which schools and partner organizations can work toward enhancing outdoor learning environments. An organized school group can effect great change very quickly, and being part of a collective energy aimed at a common task is an exhilarating experience. Perhaps the greatest value of service learning in this context is its ability to transform sterile landscapes into rich outdoor classrooms while simultaneously transforming the human beings who inhabit and shape that landscape. ❧

Mary Haque is a professor of horticulture at Clemson University in Clemson, South Carolina.

Service Learning Resources

United States

Learn and Serve America, c/o The Corporation for National Service, 1201 New York Avenue, Washington, DC 20525, (202) 606-5000, www.learnandserve.org

∗ Provides funds to service learning programs in communities, K-12 schools, colleges and universities.

National Service Learning Clearing-house, University of Minnesota, 1954 Buford Avenue, Room R460, St. Paul, MN 55108, (800) 808-7378, umn.edu/~serve

∗ Provides information about service learning to K-12 schools, colleges, and community organizations.

National Youth Leadership Council, 1910 West County Road B, St. Paul, MN 55113, (651) 631-3672, www.nylc.org

∗ A prominent advocate of service learning for young people, the council also sponsors a national conference and produces curricula and training programs for young people and adults.

Canada

There are no Canadian organizations dedicated to service learning, but community service is increasingly recognized as an important part of education. Check provincial/territorial education requirements.

Project Support and Resources

The following pages list organizations and references that can help you in planning and implementing a school grounds project. Listings are in the following order:

❧ North American organizations (national and state or provincial) that assist in the greening of school grounds by providing: funding (**F**), training (**T**), and/or publications and other resources (**R**). Where applicable, the resources available are listed after the contact information and denoted by (✷).

❧ Other recommended publications for school grounds projects.

❧ Major North American distributors of gardening and nature education resources.

ORGANIZATIONS

UNITED STATES
National Programs

Schoolyards Habitats, National Wildlife Federation, 8925 Leesburg Pike, Vienna, VA 22184, (703) 790-4582, www.nwf.org/habitats/schoolyard/. **F T R**
Regional education offices located in Seattle, San Diego, Missoula, Boulder, Austin, Atlanta, Ann Arbor, Montpelier, and Naples
✷ *Schoolyard Habitat Planning Guide; NWF's Guide to Gardening for Wildlife: How to Create a Beautiful Backyard Habitat for Birds, Butterflies, and other Wildlife*

Wild School Sites, Project WILD, 707 Conservation Lane S-305, Gaithersburg, MD 20878, (301) 527-8900, www.projectwild.org. **T R**
✷ *Wild School Sites: A Guide to Prepare for Habitat Improvement Projects on School Grounds; Exploring School Nature Areas* (video)

National Gardening Association, 1100 Dorset Street, Burlington, VT 05403, (800) 538-7476, www.kidsgardening.com. **F T R**
✷ Check web site for extensive listing of publications and other gardening resources.

Learn and Serve America, The Corporation for National Service, 1201 New York Avenue, Washington, DC 20525, (202) 606-5000, www.learnandserve.org. **F** (through state affiliates)

American Horticultural Society, Gardeners' Information Service, 7931 East Boulevard Drive, Alexandria, VA 22308-1300, (800) 777-7931 x 124, www.ahs.org. **T** (annual conference), **R**

Environmental Protection Agency, Office of Environmental Education, Washington, DC, (202) 260-4965, www.epa.gov/enviroed. **F** (through regional offices)

"Make Your World Better" Grant Program, The Center for EE, Antioch New England Graduate School, 40 Avon Street, Keene, NH 03431, (603) 357-3122, www.cee-ane.org. **F**

Resource Conservation and Community Development Division, USDA - Natural Resources Conservation Service, Washington, DC (202) 720-2847, www.rcdnet.org. **F T R** (through state offices)

Community Tree Planting Program, National Tree Trust, 1120 G Street NW, S-770, Washington, DC 20005, (800) 846-8733, www.nationaltreetrust.org. **F**

Audubon Cooperative Sanctuary Program for Schools, Audubon International, 46 Rarick Road, Selkirk, NY 12158, (518) 767-9051 x 12. **R**

Food Works, 64 Main Street, Montpelier VT 05602, (802) 223-1515. **T R**
✷ *The Indoor River Book; Digging Deeper: Integrating Youth Gardens into Schools & Communities; In the Three Sisters' Garden: Native American Stories and Seasonal Activities; The Wonderful World of Wigglers; Exploring the Forest with Grandforest Tree; Exploring the Secrets of the Meadow Thicket*

Environmental Concern, Education Dept., PO Box P, St. Michaels, MD 21663, (410) 745-9620, www.wetland.org/kids/Kids/htm. **T R**
✷ *POW! The Planning of Wetlands: An Educator's Guide; WOW! The Wonders of Wetlands; Wetland Planting Guide for the Northeastern United States*

Life Lab Science Program, 1156 High Street, Santa Cruz, CA 95064, (931) 459-2001, www.lifelab.org. **T R**
✷ *The Growing Classroom; Life Lab Science; Getting Started: A Guide for Creating School Gardens as Outdoor Classrooms*

Root and Shoots Intergenerational School Garden Program, 306 Overhill Drive, Lexington, VA 24450, (540) 463-6454, http://rootsnshoots.geo.to/. **T R**
✷ *The Down to Earth Handbook* (K-5 guide)

State Programs
Alabama

Outdoor Classrooms Program, Alabama Wildlife Federation, 46 Commerce Street, Montgomery, AL 36104, (334) 832-9453, www.alawild.org. **T R**
✷ *Outdoor Classroom and Schoolyard Habitat*

Legacy Environmental Education, 5967 Monticello Drive, Montgomery, AL 36117, (334) 270-5921, www.legacy.enved.com. **F**

Arizona

Heritage Schoolyard Habitat Grants, Arizona Fish and Game, 2221 West Greenway Road, Phoenix, AZ 85023-4312, (800) 824-2456, www.gf.state.az.us. **F T**
✷ *Schoolyard Habitat Design*

Arizona Advisory Council on Environmental Education, Arizona State Land Dept., 1616 W Adams Street, Phoenix, AZ 85007, (602) 542-2854, www.ag.arizona.edu/maricopa/garden/html/funding/aacee.htm. **F**

Maricopa County Cooperative Extension (U of A), 4341 E Broadway Road, Phoenix, AZ 85040, (480) 759-6741, www.ag.arizona.edu/maricopa/garden/html/calendar/aware.htm. **T** (conference)

Tucson Audubon, 300 East University #120, Tucson, AZ 85705, (520) 629-0510, www.azstar.com/audubon. **T R**
✷ *The Schoolyard Habitat and Garden Resource Directory*

Arkansas

Schoolyard Habitat Program, Arkansas Game and Fish Commission, 2898 Hwy 46 South, Sheridan, AR 72150, (870) 917-2085. **F T R**

California

Center for Ecoliteracy, 2522 San Pablo Avenue, Berkeley, CA 94702, (510) 845-4595, www.ecoliteracy.org. **F T R**
✷ *The Edible Schoolyard; Mapping the Terrain.*

National Wildlife Federation, 3500 Fifth Avenue, S-101, San Diego, CA 92103, (619) 296-8353. **F T R**

Center for Gardening-Based Education, Dept. of Horticulture, Plant and Soil Science, California State Polytechnic University, 3801 West Temple Avenue, Pomona, CA 91768, (909) 869-2173. **T** (conference)

California Native Plants Society, 1722 J Street, S-17, Sacramento, CA 95814, (916) 447-2677, www.cnps.org. **T R** (ask for nearest chapter)
* *Southern California Native Plants for School Gardens; Wildflowers of California* (poster series)

Leaf It To Us, California Dept. of Forestry and Fire Protection, 2524 Mulberry Street, Riverside, CA 92501, (909) 320-6125, www.ufei.calpoly.edu. **F** (tree-planting)

ReLeaf, Trust for Public Lands, 926 J Street, Sacramento, CA 95814, (916) 557-1673, www.tpl.org/cal/. **F**

Colorado
Colorado Dept. of Education, Conservation and Environmental Education, 201 East Colfax Avenue, Denver, CO 80203, (303) 291-1262. **F**

Project WILD Schoolyard Habitat Grants, Colorado Division of Wildlife, 6060 Broadway, Denver, CO 80216, (303) 814-1391, www.dnr.state.co.us/wildlife. **F**

Colorado State Forest Service, Colorado State University, 203 Forestry Building, Fort Collins, CO 80523-5060, (970) 491-6303, www.colostate.edu/Dept/CSFS/. **T**

Connecticut
Connecticut Schoolyard Habitat Network, c/o Kellogg Environmental Center, PO Box 435, Derby, CT 06418, (203) 734-2513, http://ctwoodlands.org/shn/. **T R**

Florida
Schoolyard Wildlife Project, Florida Fish and Wildlife Conservation Commission, 620 S Meridian Street, Tallahassee, FL 32399-1600, (850) 488-4679, www.state.fl.us/fwc/educator/projwild.htl. **T R**
* *Handbook to Schoolyard Plants and Animals of North Central Florida*

Florida Wildlife Federation, PO Box 6870, Tallahassee, FL 32314, (850) 656-7113, www.flawildlife.org. **T**

Georgia
Georgia Wildlife Federation, Alcovy Conservation Center, 11600 Hazelbrand Road, Covington, GA 30014, (770) 787-7887, www.gwf.org. **T R**
* *Schoolyard Wildlife Habitat Planting Guide; Schoolyard Wildlife Habitat* (video)

Outdoor Classroom Grants Program, EE Alliance of Georgia, PO Box 999, Senoia, GA 30276, www.eealliance.org. **F**

Illinois
Schoolyard Habitats Action Grants, Illinois Dept. of Natural Resources, Educational Services Section, 524 S Second Street, Room 530, Springfield, IL 62701-1787, (217) 524-4126, http://dnr.state.il.us/lands/Education/classrm/grants.htm. **F R**

St. Clair County Regional Office of Education, Director of Scientific Literacy, 500 Wilshire Drive, Belleville, IL 62223-1154, (618) 397-8930 x 133, http://web.stclair.k12.il.us/splashd/. **R**
* *Creating and Sustaining Schoolyard Habitats Instructional Unit*

Indiana
Forestry Education Program, Indiana Division of Forestry, Dept. of Natural Resources, 402 W Washington Street, Room W 296, Indianapolis, IN 46204, (317) 232-4119. **F T R**
* *Guidelines and Features for Outdoor Classrooms*

Wild School Sites, Project WILD, Natural Resources Education Center, 5785 Glenn Road, Indianapolis, IN 46216-1066, (317) 549-0348, www.state.in.us/dnr/fishwild/index.htm. **F T R**

Iowa
Iowa Conservation Education Council, PO Box 65534, West Des Moines, IA 50265, (515) 221-9893. **F T R**

Growing in the Garden, Extension 4H Youth Development, ISU, 33 Curtiss Hall, Ames, IA 50011, (515) 294-1018. **T R**
* *Growing in the Garden K-3: Growing Curiosity about Agriculture, Natural Resources, Food and People; Growing in the Garden: Outdoor Classrooms for Young Gardeners*

Iowa Department of Education, Environmental Ed. Consultant, Grimes State Office Bldg, Des Moines, IA 50319, (515) 281-3146. **T**

Kid's Connections, 28658 Tonka Place, New Hartford, IA 50660, (319) 983-2622. **T R**

Kansas
Kansas Assoc. for Conservation and Environmental Education, 2610 Claflin, Manhattan, KS 66502, (785) 532-3322, www.kacee.org. **F T**

Outdoor Wildlife Learning Sites, Kansas Dept. of Wildlife and Parks, 512 SE 25th Avenue, Pratt, KS 67124, (316) 672-5911 x 151 or 108, www.kdwp.state.ks.us. **F T R**

Kentucky
Kentucky Environmental Education Council, 1705 Capital Plaza Tower, Frankfort, KY 40601, (502) 564-5937, www.state.ky.us/agencies/envred/. **T F**

Kentucky Department of Fish and Wildlife Resources, Wildlife Education Administrator, 1 Game Farm Rd., Frankfort, KY 40601, (800) 858-1549. **T**

Urban Forestry Grant Program, Kentucky Division of Forestry, 627 Comanche Trail, Frankfort, KY 40601, (502) 564-4496, www.nr.state.ky.us/nrepc/dnr/forestry/dnrdof. **F** (for trees)

Maryland
Schoolyard Habitat Program, US Fish and Wildlife Service, 177 Admiral Cochrane Drive, Annapolis, MD 21401, (410) 573-4584, www.fws.gov/r5cbfo/schoolyd.htm. **R**
* *Schoolyard Habitat Project Guide*

Chesapeake Bay Trust, 60 West Street, S-200A, Annapolis, MD 21401, (410) 974-2941, www.cbtrust.org. **F** (in CB watershed)

Education Coordinator, Maryland Dept. of Natural Resources, Tawes Bldg E-2, 580 Taylor Avenue, Annapolis, MD 21401, (410) 260-8710, www.dnr.state.md.us/education/teacherslounge. **F** (aquatic projects)

Massachusetts
The Arnold Arboretum, 125 Arborway, Jamaica Plain, MA 02130-3519, (617) 524-1718 x 109, www.arboretum.harvard.edu. **T R**
* *Teachers' Guide; Seasonal Investigations of Trees*

Boston Schoolyard Funders Collaborative, Boston Foundation, 1 Boston Place, 24th Floor, Boston, MA 02108, (617) 723-7415, www.schoolyards.org. **T R F**

Michigan

National Wildlife Federation, Great Lakes Natural Resource Center, 506 E Liberty Street, 2nd Floor, Ann Arbor, MI 48104, (734) 769-3351. **F T R**

Nature Education Sites for Tomorrow, Director of Wildlife Programs, Michigan Wildlife Habitat Foundation, PO Box 393, Bath, MI 48808, (517) 641-7677, www.mwhf.org. **F T R**

Wildlife Division, Natural Heritage Unit, Michigan Dept. of Natural Resources, Box 30180, Lansing, MI 48909, (517) 373-2457, www.dnr.state.mi.us. **F**

Minnesota

School Nature Area Project, St. Olaf College, 1520 St. Olaf Avenue, Northfield, MN 55057, (507) 646-3977, www.stolaf.edu/other/snap/. **F T R**
* *Exploring School Nature Areas* (video); *Homes for Wildlife: A Planning Guide for Habitat Enhancement on School Grounds; Learning Under the Sun* (video); *Minnesota School Nature Areas: Notes on Benefitting the Biomes*

Mississippi

Mississippi State Extension Service, Desoto County, 3260 Hwy 51 South, Hernando, MS 38632, (662) 429-1343, www.ext.msstate.edu. **T R**

Community Pride Project, 402 Bost, Box 9641, Mississippi State, MS 39762-9641, (662) 325-1691. **F**

Missouri

Missouri State Department of Conservation, Education Services, PO Box 180, Jefferson City, MO 65102, (573) 751-4155 x 3295, www.conservation.state.mo.us/teacher/outdoor/. **F T R**
* *A Guide to the Planning and Development of Outdoor Classrooms*

Gateway Greening Inc., PO Box 299, St. Louis, MO 63166, (314) 577-9484, www.gatewaygreening.org. **T R** (St. Louis area)

Montana

National Wildlife Federation, 240 North Higgins, S-2, Missoula, MT 59802, (406) 721-6705. **F T R**

Montana Partners in Ecology, Division of Biological Sciences, U of Montana, Missoula, MT 59812, (406) 243-6016, http://ibscore.dbs.umt.edu/pie. **T**

New Hampshire

Project Home, NH Fish and Game Education Unit, 2 Hazen Drive, Concord, NH 03301, (603) 271-3211, www.wildlife.stat.nh.us. **T R**
* *Homes for Wildlife: A Planning Guide for Habitat Enhancement on School Grounds*

New Jersey

Coalition for Schoolyard Habitats, Alliance for New Jersey EE, PO Box 693, Bernardsville, NJ 07924, (908) 766-5787, www.eenj.rutgers.edu. **T R**

Project WILD, DEQ, Division of Fish and Wildlife, Pequest Trout Hatchery, 650 Pequest Road, Oxford, NJ 07863, (908) 637-4125, www.eenj.rutgers.edu. **T R**

New Mexico

NM State Land Office, PO Box 1148, Santa Fe, NM 87504-1148, (505) 827-5764. **T R**

4H Seeds Project, Cooperative Extension, 1510 Menaul NW, Albuquerque, NM 87107, (505) 243-1386, www.cahe.nmsu.edu/bernalillo. **T R**

NM Conservation Districts, 163 Trail Canyon Road, Carlsbad, NM 88220, (505) 981-2400, www.nm.nacdnet.org.**R**

New York

New York Department of Environmental Conservation: four regional EE centers offer training: (Mid-Hudson and South) Stony Kill EE Center, Wappingers Falls, (845) 831-8780; (Catskills West) Rogers EE Center, Sherburne, (607) 674-4017; (the Capitol) Five Rivers EE Center, Delmar, (518) 457-0291; (Long Island) Quoque Wildlife Sanctuary, Quogue, (631) 653-4771. **T**

Roger Tory Peterson Institute, Education Dept., 311 Curtis Street, Jamestown, NY 14701, (716) 665-2473. **T**

Institute of Ecosystem Studies, Education Programs, Box R, Millbrook, NY 12545-0178, (845) 677-7600, www.ecostudies.org. **T R**
* *Eco-Inquiry* (curriculum)

North Carolina

Using the Outdoors to Teach Experiential Science, NC Museum of Natural Sciences, 11 W Jones Street, Raleigh, NC 27626, (919) 733-7450 x 621/620, www.naturalsciences.org. **F T R**
* *Nature Neighborhood* (video); *Plant It and They Will Come: Using Native Trees and Shrubs to Attract Wildlife*

Ohio

Habitats for Learning, Ohio Dept. of Natural Resources, Division of Soil and Water Conservation, EE Section, 1939 Fountain Square Court, B E-2, Columbus, OH 43224, (614) 265-6878. **T R**
* *Habitats for Learning: A Planning Guide for Using and Developing School Land Labs; Habitats for Learning: Ohio Takes a New Look at School Land Labs* (video); *Habitats for Learning: Directory of (Ohio) School Land Labs*

Ohio (EPA) Environmental Education Fund, Lazarus Government Center, PO Box 1049, Columbus, OH 43216-1049, (614) 644-2873, www.epa.ohio.gov/other/oeemain.html. **F**

Parkworks, 1836 Euclid Avenue, S-800, Cleveland, OH 44115, (216) 696-2122 x 116. **T R**
* *Green Schools Guide; The Moon Unit*

Cleveland Botanical Garden, 11030 East Boulevard, Cleveland, OH 44106, (216) 721-1600, www.cbgarden.org. **T** (two annual symposia)

Oklahoma

Environmental Education, Dept. of Environmental Quality, PO Box 1677, Oklahoma City, OK 73101-1677, (405) 702-5166, www.deq.state.ok.us. **F T R**

Project WILD, Oklahoma Dept. of Wildlife Conservation, 1801 N Lincoln, Oklahoma City, OK 73105-4998, (405) 521-4636. **F**

The Center for Environmental Education, Oklahoma State University, 402 Willard, Stillwater, OK 74078, (405) 744-7233, home.okstate.edu/homepages.nfs/toc/cee-osu. **R**

Partners for Fish and Wildlife, US Fish and Wildlife, 222 South Houston S-A, Tulsa, OK 74127, (918) 581-7458 x 231. **F R**

Oregon

Oregon State University Extension Service, 4H Urban Natural Resources, 404 SE 80th Avenue, Portland, OR 97215, (503) 725-2046. **T** (for parent volunteers), **R**

Pennsylvania

Project WILD, Pennsylvania Game Commission, 2001 Elmerton Avenue, Harrisburg, PA 17110, (717) 783-4872. **F T R**
* *Homes for Wildlife: Pennsylvania Adaptation*

Environmental Education Grants Program, Pennsylvania Dept. of Environmental Protection, PO Box 8454, Harrisburg, PA 17105-8454, (717) 772-1828, www.dep.state.pa.us. **F**

Pennsylvania Audubon, 100 Wildwood Way, Harrisburg, PA 17112, (717) 213-6880. **T R**
❋ *APATH: Native Plants and the Creation of Backyards, Schoolyards and Park Habitat Areas*

Audubon Society of Western Pennsylvania, 614 Dorseyville Road, Pittsburgh, PA 15238, (412) 963-6100, www.aswp.org, **T R**

Alliance for Chesapeake Bay, 600 North Second, S-300B, Harrisburg, PA 17101, (717) 236-8825, www.acb-online.org. **T R**

Rhode Island
Southern Rhode Island Conservation District, 60 Quaker Lane, S-46, Warwick, RI 02886-1114, (401) 822-8832, www.sricd.org. **T R**

South Carolina
South Carolina Landscapes for Learning Collaborative, Dept. of Sociology, Brackett 132, Box 341356, Clemson University, Clemson, SC 29634-1356, (864) 656-3821, http://people.clemson.edu/~vanmey/lfl.htm. **F T R**
❋ *Resources for Gardening with Children and Youth*

Tennessee
Center for Environmental Education, Middle Tennessee State University, Murfreesboro, TN 37132, (615) 898-5449. **F T**

Tennessee EE Association, c/o Great Smoky Mountains Institute at Tremont, 9275 Tremont Road, Townsend, TN 37882, (865) 448-6709, www.utm.edu/departments/ed/cece/teea.html. **F**

Center for Environmental and Conservation Education, U of T at Martin, 239 Gooch, Martin, TN 38238, (901) 587-7200, www.utm.edu/departments/ed/cece/cece.html. **T**

Texas
Wildlife Diversity Program, Texas Parks and Wildlife Dept., 4200 Smith School Road, Austin, TX 78744, (800) 792-1112, www.tpwd.state.tx.us/nature/wildscapes/. **T R** (via local offices)
❋ *Creating a School Habitat in Texas; Texas Wildscapes: Gardening for Wildlife*

National Wildlife Federation, Gulf States Office, 44 East Avenue, S-200, Austin, TX 78701, (512) 476-9805. **F T R**

Utah
Leaf It To Us (tree-planting) and **Outdoor Classroom Development Programs**, Utah Division of Forestry, Fire and State Lands, PO Box 145703, Salt Lake City, UT 84114, (801) 538-5505. **F T R**
❋ *Arbor Month Guide* (K-6)

Naturescaping School Grants, Utah Division of Wildlife Resources, 1594 West North Temple, S-2110, Salt Lake City, UT 84116, (801) 538-4719, www.nr.state.ut.us/dwr/!proj0.htm. **F**

Utah Society for Environmental Education, 350 South 400 East Street G4, Salt Lake City, UT 84111, (801) 328-1549, www.usee.org. **T R**

Vermont
Schoolyard Habitats, National Wildlife Federation, 58 State Street, Montpelier, VT 05602, (802) 229-0650. **F T R**

Vermont Institute of Natural Science, RR 2 Box 532, Woodstock, VT 05091, (802) 457-2779. **T**

Virginia
Wild School Sites, Project WILD, Virginia Dept. of Game and Inland Fisheries, 4010 W Broad Street, Richmond, VA 23230-1104, (804) 367-6989, www.dgif.state.va.us. **T**

Virginia Museum of Natural History, Education Dept., 1001 Douglas Avenue, Martinsville, VI 24112, (540) 666-8609, www.vmnh.org. **T R**
❋ *The Model Inquiries Into Nature in the Schoolyard (MINTS) Book; Gardening For Nature: A Teacher's Guide to Hands-On Activities for Wildlife Gardening*

Virginia Environmental Endowment, Three James Center, PO Box 790, Richmond, VA 23218, (804) 644-5000, www.vee.org. **F**

Arlingtonians for a Clean Environment, 3308 Stafford Street S, Arlington, VA 22206, (703) 228-6427. **T**

Washington
National Wildlife Federation, 418 1st Avenue W, Seattle, WA 98119, (206) 285-8707. **F T**

Wisconsin
Earth Partnership Program, UW-Arboretum, 1207 Seminole Hwy, Madison, WI 53711, (608) 262-5522, www.wisc.edu/arboretum. **T R**
❋ *Prairie Restoration for Wisconsin Schools; A Prairie Journey* (slide show); *A Prairie Journey* (video)

CANADA
National Programs
Toyota Evergreen Learning Grounds Program, c/o Evergreen, 355 Adelaide Street W, 5th floor, Toronto, ON M5V 1S2, (888) 426-3138, www.evergreen.ca. **F T R**
❋ *A Crack in the Pavement* (2-video set); *All Hands in the Dirt: A Guide to Designing and Creating Natural School Grounds; Grounds For Change* (video); *Nature Nurtures: Investigating the Potential of School Grounds; Stewards and Storytellers: The Greening of British Columbia School Grounds*

Habitat 2000 and **Wild Education**, Canadian Wildlife Federation, 350 Michael Cowpland Drive, Kanata, ON K2M 2W1, (800) 563-WILD, www.cwf-fcf.org, www.wildeducation.org. **F T R**

Greening Canada's School Grounds, Tree Canada Foundation, 220 Laurier Avenue W, S-1550, Ottawa, ON K1P 5Z9, (613) 567-5545, www.treecanada.ca. **F T R**

Canadian Biodiversity Institute, 99 Fifth Avenue, S-322, Ottawa, ON K1S 5P5, (613) 826-2190, www.biodiversityonline.ca. **T R**

Environment Canada EcoAction program (through regional offices), (800) 663-5755, www.ec.gc.ca/ecoaction/. **F**

Canada Trust Friends of the Environment Foundation, (800) 361-5333, www.fef.ca. **F**

Shell Environmental Fund, (800) 338-1410, www.shell.ca/people.htm. **F**

Provincial/Territorial Programs
Alberta
Grounds for Change - Schoolyard Naturalization Project, Calgary Zoo, PO Box 3036 Stn B, Calgary, AB T2M 4R8, www.calgaryzoo.ab.ca. **T**

Naturescape Alberta, PO Box 785, Red Deer, AB T4N 5H2, (403) 347-8200, www.naturescape.ab.ca. **R**

Devonian Botanic Garden, University of Alberta, Edmonton, AB T6G 2E1, (780) 987-3054, www.discoveredmonton.com/devonian. **T R**

132

British Columbia

Evergreen West, 410 - 744 W Hastings Street, Vancouver, BC V6C 1A5, (604) 689-0766, www.evergreen.ca. **F T R**
❀ *Plants, Patterns and Playgrounds; BC Resource Guide 2000; Stewards and Storytellers: The Greening of British Columbia School Grounds*

Greening Schoolgrounds, 1836 McNicoll Avenue, Vancouver, BC V6J 1A4, www.greengrounds.ca. **T R**
❀ *Landscapes for Learning* (guide)

Habitat Conservation Trust Fund, Ministry of Environment, Lands and Parks, PO Box 9354, Stn Prov Govt, Victoria, BC V9W 9M1, (800) 387-9853, www.env.gov.bc.ca. **F T R**
❀ *Naturescape Kit; Backyard Biodiversity and Beyond* (also available in French)

Douglas College Habitat Restoration Program, PO Box 2503, New Westminster, BC V3L 5B2, (604) 527-5817, www.douglas.bc.ca/envcentre. **T**

City Farmer, 2150 Maple Street, Vancouver, BC V6J 3T3, (604) 685-5832, www.cityfarmer.org. **T R**
❀ *School Garden Guidelines: How to Teach Children About Nutrition and the Environment; Urban Home Composting: Rodent-Resistant Bins and Environmental Health Standards*

Manitoba

The Fort Whyte Centre, 1961 McCreary Road, Winnipeg, MB R3P 2K9, (204) 989-8355, www.fortwhyte.org. **F** (Winnipeg only)

Living Prairie Museum, 2795 Ness Avenue, Winnipeg, MB R3J 3S4, (204) 832-0167, www.city.winnipeg.mb.ca/cms-prod/parks/envserv/interp/liv. **T R**

New Brunswick

Falls Brook Centre, 125 S Knowlesville Road, Knowlesville, NB E7L 1B1, (506) 375-8143, www.web.net/~fbcja. **T R**
❀ *Bringing Nature Back To School*

Ontario

Federation of Ontario Naturalists, 355 Lesmill Road, Don Mills, ON M3B 2W8, (800) 440-2366, www.ontarionature.org. **T R**

The Arboretum, University of Guelph, Guelph, ON N1G 3W1, (519) 824-4120 x 6443, www.uoguelph.ca/~arboretum. **T R**

Royal Botanical Gardens, PO Box 399, Hamilton, ON L8N 3H8, (905) 527-1158, www.rbg.ca. **T R**

Ontario Society for Environmental Education, 700 Frederick Street, Kitchener, ON N2B 2B2, (519) 744-7918, www.osee.org. **T**

School Peace Gardens, 3343 Masthead Crescent, Mississauga, ON L5L 1G9, (905) 820-5067, www.pathcom.com/~ihtec. **T**

LIFE-SPIN, PO Box 2801, London, ON N6A 4H4, (519) 438-8676, www.execulink.com/~life. **T R**
❀ *Pocket-Sized Farms - Kid's Gardening Book; Pocket-Sized Farms - Teaching and Planning Guide*

Québec

La Société de l'arbre du Québec, 1055 rue du PEPS, CP 3800, Ste. Foy, QC G1V 4C7, (819) 648-5699, www.sodaq.qc.ca. **F R**
❀ *ABC de la plantation d'arbres: Guide pour la réalisation de projets de plantation en milieu scolaire*

Saskatchewan

Saskatchewan Outdoor and Environmental Education Association, (306) 586-8875, www.sympatico.sk.ca/kathyh. **F**

Yukon

Conservation Education, Dept. of Renewable Resources, Government of Yukon, Box 2703 (R-7), Whitehorse, YT Y1A 2C6, (867) 667-3675. **R**

OTHER RECOMMENDED RESOURCES

Outdoor Classrooms: Rationale

Nabhan, Gary, and Stephen Trimble. *The Geography of Childhood.* Boston: Beacon Press, 1994, ISBN 0-8070-8525-1.

Rivkin, Mary S. *The Great Outdoors: Restoring Children's Right to Play Outside.* Washington: National Association for the Education of Young Children, 1995, ISBN 0-935989-71-4. Orders: (202) 232-8777 x 2001.

Sobel, David. *Children's Special Places: Exploring the Role of Forts, Dens and Bush Houses in Middle Childhood.* Tucson: Zephyr Press, 1993, ISBN 0-913705-81-0. Orders: (800) 232-2187.

Planning and Implementation

Abend, Allen C., Gary Heath and Richard Mason, eds. *Conserving and Enhancing the Natural Environment: A Guide for Planning, Design, Construction, and Maintenance on New and Existing School Sites.* Baltimore: Maryland State Department of Education, 1999, no ISBN. Orders: (410) 767-0098, www.msde.state.md.us.

Arbury, Jim. *The Complete Book of Plant Propagation.* Newtown, CT: Taunton Press, 1997, ISBN 1-56158-234-4. Orders: (800) 243-7252, www.taunton.com.

Bar, Laurel and Judith Galluzzo. *The Accessible School: Universal Design for Educational Settings.* Berkeley, CA: MIG Communications, 1996, ISBN 0-94466-120-3. Orders: (800) 790-8444, www.migcom.com.

Cheskey, Edward D. *Habitat Restoration: A Guide for Proactive Schools.* Kitchener, ON: Waterloo Region District School Board, 1993, Product #93-14027, no ISBN. Orders: WRDSB Learning Resources Dept., (519) 570-0300 x 4339.

Gosselin, Heather M. and Bob R. Johnson. *The Urban Outback — Wetlands for Wildlife: A Guide to Wetland Restoration and Frog-friendly Backyards.* Toronto: Metro Toronto Zoo Adopt-a-Pond, 1995, ISBN 1-89574-102-5. Orders: (416) 392-5999, www.torontozoo.com.

Henderson, Carrol L. *Lakescaping for Wildlife and Water Quality.* St. Paul: Minnesota's Bookstore, 1999, ISBN 0-96474-512-7. Orders: (651) 297-3000.

———. *Landscaping for Wildlife.* St. Paul: Minnesota's Bookstore, 1994, no ISBN. Orders: (651) 297-3000.

———. *Woodworking for Wildlife.* St. Paul: Minnesota's Bookstore, 1992, no ISBN. Orders: (651) 297-3000.

Hunter, Jane, Julie Laywell, and Nicola Rogers. *School Landscapes: A Participatory Approach to Design.* Winchester: Hampton County Council, 1998, ISBN 1-85975-201-2. Orders: (800) 473-3638, http://gbr.org.

Johns, Frank A., Kurt Allen Liske, and Amy L. Evans. *Education Goes Outdoors.* Menlo Park: Addison-Wesley, 1986, ISBN 0-20120-471-1. Orders: (800) 848-9500, www.aw.com.

Johnson, Lorraine. *Grow Wild! Native Plant Gardening in Canada and Northern United States.* Mississauga: Random House of Canada, 1998, ISBN 0-67930-919-5. Orders (800) 668-4247, www.randomhouse.ca.

133

Martin, Deborah, Bill Lucas, Wendy Titman, and Siobhan Hayward, eds. *Challenge of the Urban School Site.* Winchester, UK: Learning through Landscapes, 1996, ISBN 1-87286-516-X. Orders: Green Brick Road, (800) 473-3638, http://gbr.org.

McIntyre, Sally and Susan M. Goltsman. *Safety First Checklist: Audit and Inspection Program for Children's Play Areas.* Berkeley, CA: MIG Communications, 1997, ISBN 0-94466-119-X. Orders: (800) 790-8444, www.migcom.com.

Mikula, Rick. *The Family Butterfly Book.* Pownal, VT: Storey Communications, 2000, ISBN 1-58017-292-X. Orders: (802) 823-5810, www.storey.com.

Minno, Marc C., and Maria Minno. *Florida Butterfly Gardening: A Complete Guide to Attracting, Identifying and Enjoying Butterflies of the Lower South.* Gainesville: University Press of Florida, 1999, ISBN 0-81301-665-7. Orders: (352) 392-1351, www.upf.com.

Moore, Robin C., Susan M. Goltsman, and Daniel S. Iacofano, eds. *Play for All Guidelines: Planning, Design and Management of Outdoor Play Settings for All Children.* Berkeley, CA: MIG Communications, 1992, ISBN 0-94466-117-3. Orders: (800) 790-8444, www.migcom.com.

Moore, Robin C., and Herb H. Wong. *Natural Learning: The Life History of an Environmental Schoolyard.* Berkeley, CA: MIG Communications, 1997, ISBN 0-94466-124-6. Orders: (800) 790-8444, www.migcom.com.

Packard, Stephan, and Cornelia Mutel, eds. *The Tallgrass Restoration Handbook for Prairies, Savannas, and Woodlands.* Washington, DC: Island Press, 1996, ISBN 1-55963-320-4. Orders: (800) 828-1302, www.islandpress.org.

Pennington, Gary, and Aline Wilkie. *Welcoming Back the Wilderness: Impact of a School Naturalization Project Upon a School and Its Community.* Saskatoon: Dr. Stirling McDowell Foundation for Research into Teaching, 1999, no ISBN. Orders: Teaching and Learning Research Exchange, Saskatchewan Teachers' Federation, (800) 667-7762, www.stf.sk.ca.

Prairie Seed Source. *Prairie Restoration for the Beginner.* Franklin, WI: Wehr Nature Center, 1995, no ISBN. Orders: (414) 425-8550, www.uwm.edu/Dept/Biology/Wehr/.

Rock, Harold W. *Prairie Propagation Handbook,* Franklin, WI: Wehr Nature Center, 1981, no ISBN. Orders: (414) 425-8550, www.uwm.edu/Dept/Biology/Wehr/.

Rowe, Susan. *The Seasons in the School Grounds.* Winchester, UK: Learning through Landscapes, 1991, no ISBN. Orders: Green Brick Road, (800) 473-3638, http://gbr.org.

Stine, Sharon. *Environments for Children and Youth.* John Wiley & Sons, 1996, ISBN 0-471-16222-1. Orders: U.S. (800) 225-5945, Canada (800) 567-4797, www.wiley.com.

Stoneham, Jane. *Grounds for Sharing.* Winchester, UK: Learning through Landscapes, 1996, ISBN 1-87286-523-2. Orders: Green Brick Road, (800) 473-3638, http://gbr.org.

Texas Agricultural Extension Service. *Junior Master Gardener Handbook (Level 1),* ISBN 0-9672990-0-4; *Junior Master Gardener Teacher/Leader Guide (Level 1),* ISBN 0-96729-901-2. College Station: Texas Agricultural Extension Service, 1999. Orders: Agricultural Communications, (979) 845-2211.

Titman, Wendy. *Special Places, Special People: The Hidden Curriculum of School Grounds.* Winchester, UK: Learning through Landscapes, 1994, ISBN 0-94761-348-X. Orders: Green Brick Road, (800) 473-3638, http://gbr.org.

Turner, Carole B. *Seed Sowing and Saving.* Pownal, VT: Storey Communications, 1998, ISBN 1-58017-001-3. Orders: (802) 823-5810, www.storey.com.

Williams, Sara. *Creating the Prairie Xeriscape: Low-maintenance, Water Efficient Gardening.* Saskatoon: University of Saskatchewan, 1997, ISBN 0-88880-357-5. Orders: (306) 966-5565, www.extension.usask.ca/.

Outdoor Classroom Curricula

Chedzoy, Sue. *Physical Education in the School Grounds: Learning through Landscapes.* UK: Southgate, 2000, ISBN 1-85741-012-2. Orders: Green Brick Road, (800) 473-3638, http://gbr.org.

Dean, Jacqui. *History in the School Grounds: Learning through Landscapes.* UK: Southgate, 1999, ISBN 1-85741-002-5. Orders: Green Brick Road, (800) 473-3638, http://gbr.org.

Hare, Ralph, Christine Attenborough, and Trevor Day. *Geography in the School Grounds: Learning through Landscapes.* UK: Southgate, 1996, ISBN 1-85741-023-8. Orders: Green Brick Road, (800) 473-3638, http://gbr.org.

Keaney, Brian. *Arts in the School Grounds: Learning through Landscapes.* UK: Southgate, 1996, ISBN 1-85741-036-X. Orders: Green Brick Road, (800) 473-3638, http://gbr.org.

———. *English in the School Grounds: Learning through Landscapes.* UK: Southgate, 1996, ISBN 1-85741-031-9. Orders: Green Brick Road, (800) 473-3638, http://gbr.org.

Rhydderch-Evans, Zoe. *Mathematics in the School Grounds: Learning through Landscapes.* UK: Southgate, 1993, ISBN 1-85741-021-1. Orders: Green Brick Road, (800) 473-3638, http://gbr.org.

Russell, Helen Ross. *Ten-Minute Field Trips: A Teacher's Guide to Using the School Grounds for Environmental Studies.* Washington: National Science Teacher's Association, 1990, ISBN 0-87355-098-6. Orders: (800) 722-6782, www.nsta.org.

Thomas, Gill. *Science in the School Grounds: Learning through Landscapes.* UK: Southgate, 1992, ISBN 1-85741-085-8. Orders: Green Brick Road, (800) 473-3638, http://gbr.org.

Thomson, Gareth, and Sue Arlidge. *Five-Minute Field Trips: Teaching About Nature in Your Schoolyard.* Edmonton: Alberta Teachers' Association/Calgary Zoo, 2000, no ISBN. Orders: ATA, (780) 447-9400.

SOURCES/DISTRIBUTORS

Acorn Naturalists, East 17th Street, S-103, PO Box 2423, Tustin, CA 92781-2423, (800) 422-8886, www.acornnaturalists.com.
✱ Largest North American distributor of natural science education resources. Free catalog.

Green Brick Road, 429 Danforth Avenue, S-408, Toronto, ON M4K 1P1, (800) 473-3638, http://gbr.org.
✱ North American distributor of the highly-regarded Learning through Landscapes titles from Great Britain.

Let's Get Growing, 1900 Commercial Way, Santa Cruz, CA 95065, (800) 408-1868, www.letsgetgrowing.com.
✱ Largest North American distributor of resources for school gardening. Free catalog.

Project Support and Resources

Index

Administrators, getting support of, 17, 20
Algal growth, in ponds, 70
Amphibians, pond construction, 66-70
Audits, see site assessment

Behavior, effect of school grounds on, 3, 5-8
Benches, 32, 39, 82
Biodiversity inventory, 29
Birds
    birdbaths, 73, 76
    feeders, 39, 71-73, 84
    food sources, 72, 75
    nesting boxes, 72, 75, 84
    providing habitat for, 71-76
    related curriculum, 73-74
Boardwalks, 83
Bridges, 83
Butterfly gardens, 77-79

Caterpillars, 78
Chlorine, in ponds, 69
Community participation, 18, 25
Composting, 93-97
Contest, Ugliest School Yard, 23-24
Cross-curricular studies, high school 35
Curriculum, see Curriculum Index, 136
Custodians, 17

Decomposition, experiment, 94
Desert and dryland gardens, 51-53
Design of projects, 31-33
    amphibian ponds, 66-67
    benches, tables, 82-85
    butterfly gardens, 78
    desert and dryland gardens, 51-52
    natural wetlands, 45
    prairie restoration, 48
    to-scale models, 29-33
Desire lines, 29
Donations, 20, 26, 28
Dyes, natural, 116

Ecological restoration
    definition of, 46
    environmental values and, 10
    natural succession, 40-42
    prairie, 46-50
Educational benefits of school grounds, 9-10
Environmental ethics, 12

Field guide, creating, 104-105
Fences, 31, 38
Food, for birds, 72, 75
    gardens, 122-123
Fundraising, 19-22, 23, 26, 102-103

Gardens
    butterfly, 77-79
    desert and dryland, 51-53
    multicultural, 122-123
    prairie, 46-50
    rooftop, 57-59
    vegetable, 100, 122
    wildlife habitat, 65
Germination, K-6 experiments, 102
Grants (fundraising), 20-21

High schools, greening, 34-36
History, school grounds greening, 3

Landscape, innate preferences in, 7
Lawns, aerating and dressing, 28
Leafprinting, 117
Lumber, choice of, 82

Maintenance
    of planted sites, 26, 28, 79, 89, 102
    of prairie plantings, 49-50
Maintenance staff, 17
Master plan, 19, see also site plan
Meadows, 38, 40,
Media coverage, 21
Model-making, 29-33
Mulch, 28, 48, 79
Multicultural gardens, 122-123
Mystery, as an element of landscape, 7

Native plants
    as food sources for birds, 72
    importance to wildlife, 64-65
    selection of, 27, 41, 45, 65, 77-78
Natural succession, 40
Nest boxes, 39, 72, 75, 84
Nursery, tree, 54-56

Papermaking, 117
Parents, involvement in projects, 18, 82
Paths and trails, 28, 83-84
Planning, see design, site selection, project team
Plant list, 27, see also native plants
Ponds
    designing for amphibians, 66-70
    liners for, 66-67, 69
    maintaining, 70
    overflow, 44, 67
    retention or seasonal, 43-45
    safety of, 68, 87-88
Prairie
    management of, 49-50
    restoration of, 46-50
    curriculum related to, 114-115
Project team, 16-18, 25

Raised growing beds, 55
Research
    educational benefits of school ground greening, 9-11
    psychological effect of physical surroundings, 5-8
Rocks, as design features, 39, 53
Rooftop gardens, 57-59
Root zone, protection of, 41, 117

Safety
    of ponds, 87-88
    of rooftop gardens, 58
    from vandalism, 89-92
Seating, 32, 39, 82
Seed collection, 41, 49, 55
Service learning, 34, 127-128
Shade audit, 30

Shelters, sun, 86
Sight lines, 32
Signage, 89
Site assessment and selection,
  26, 29-31
    butterfly gardens, 77
    retention ponds, 43-44
    prairie restorations, 48
    amphibian ponds, 66
Soil
    determining type, 44
    estimating permeability of, 44
    preparing for planting, 27, 48
Students, involvement in projects,
  10, 16
Succession, natural, 40
Sun shelters, 86
Surface-water runoff, 43
Surveillance of school grounds,
  5, 32, 90
Surveys, see site assessment

Tables and benches, 82
Trails, 28, 83-84
Trees
    care of, 41-42, 55-56
    growing from seed, 55-56
    as habitat for wildlife, 38
    models of, 30
    rethinking tree-planting, 40-42
    protective baskets, 117
    schoolyard tree nursery, 54-56
    seed collection, 55

Vandalism, discouraging, 89-92
Vegetable gardens, 12-14, 39, 100
Vermicomposting, 96
Vernal ponds, 43-45
Volunteers, recruiting and
    organizing, 18, 26-27

Waste management, by
    composting, 93-97

Water
    for attracting wildlife, 75
    estimating volume on school
        grounds, 44
    humans' innate preference for, 7
    pond overflows, 67
    retention ponds, 43-45, 66
    surface runoff, 43
Weeds, removal of, 48
Wetlands, 38, 43-45, 66-70
Wildlife, see also amphibians, birds,
    butterflies
    creating habitat for, 62-81, 75
    children's alienation from,
        62-63
    co-evolution with native
        plants, 64
    corridors, 41, 72
Worm composting, 96

Xeriscaping, desert gardens, 51-53

Curriculum Index

Subject	Grades K-3	Grades 4-6	Grades 7-8	Grades 9-12
Art	103, 110, 114, 116, 117	89, 101, 103, 104, 106, 108, 111, 114, 116, 117	89, 104, 112, 115, 116, 117	34, 89, 104, 115, 116, 117
Health / Physical Education		95, 106, 108	95	35, 95
Home Economics		108	108, 113	108, 113
Language Arts	107, 111, 114	16, 17, 47, 89, 106, 111, 114, 115	16, 17, 47, 89, 112, 115	17, 35, 47, 89, 113, 115
Mathematics	110, 114, 119, 120	17, 65, 74, 106, 107, 111, 114, 115, 119, 121	17, 65, 74, 115, 119, 120, 121	35, 74, 113, 115, 119, 120
Music	114	95, 109, 114	95	95, 115
Science	17, 53, 65, 74, 93, 96, 102, 103, 110, 114	17, 48, 53, 65, 74, 94, 96, 101, 102, 103, 104, 106, 108, 111, 114-115	17, 48, 53, 65, 74, 94, 104, 112, 115	35, 48, 53, 65, 74
Social Studies	111	47, 53, 65, 108, 111, 114, 115, 122, 123	47, 53, 65, 95, 112, 115, 122	35, 47, 53, 65, 95, 115, 122